DATE DUE

"Jan evokes a great longing and hunger to know Jesu encouraging us to stop and listen, not wanting t word He has to say. She brings us face-to-face ever-present Jesus, reminding us of His greatne and waiting for us to love Him in return. This b ates a deep desire to share our daily life with Hin

—KATHLEEN HART, speaker, author and chaplain t wives at Fuller Theological

WHEN THE SOUL LISTENS

FINDING REST AND DIRECTION IN CONTEMPLATIVE PRAYER

JAN JOHNSON

NAVPRESS
BRINGING TRUTH TO LIFE
P.O. Box 35001, Colorado Springs, Colorado 80935

OUR GUARANTEE TO YOU

We believe so strongly in the message of our books that we are making this quality guarantee to you. If for any reason you are disappointed with the content of this book, return the title page to us with your name and address and we will refund to you the list price of the book. To help us serve you better, please briefly describe why you were disappointed. Mail your refund request to: NavPress, P.O. Box 35002, Colorado Springs, CO 80935.

The Navigators is an international Christian organization. Our mission is to reach, disciple, and equip people to know Christ and to make Him known through successive generations. We envision multitudes of diverse people in the United States and every other nation who have a passionate love for Christ, live a lifestyle of sharing Christ's love, and multiply spiritual laborers among those without Christ.

NavPress is the publishing ministry of The Navigators. NavPress publications help believers learn biblical truth and apply what they learn to their lives and ministries. Our mission is to stimulate spiritual formation among our readers.

Library of Congress Catalog Card Number: 99-41040
ISBN 1-57683-113-2

Cover design by Dan Jamison
Photo by Brian Fraunfelter/The StockRep, Inc.

Some of the anecdotal illustrations in this book are true to life and are included with the permission of the persons involved. All other illustrations are composites of real situations, and any resemblance to people living or dead is coincidental.

Unless otherwise identified, all Scripture quotations in this publication are taken from the *Holy Bible: New International Version* ® (NIV®). Copyright © 1973, 1978, 1984 by International Bible Society. Used by permission of Zondervan Publishing House. All rights reserved. Other versions used include: the *New King James Version* (NKJV), copyright ©1979, 1980, 1982, 1990, Thomas Nelson Inc., Publishers; and the *King James Version* (KJV).

Johnson, Jan, 1947–
      When the soul listens : finding rest and direction in contemplative
prayer / Jan Johnson.
      p. cm.
      Includes bibliographical references.
      ISBN 1-57683-113-2 (pbk.)
      1. Meditation —Christianity.   2. Prayer—Christianity   I. Title
BV4813.J62 1999
248.3'4 — dc21   99-41040
                                                                                CIP

Printed in the United States of America

2 3 4 5 6 7 8 9 10 11 12 / 05 04 03 02 01 00

FOR A FREE CATALOG OF
NAVPRESS BOOKS & BIBLE STUDIES,
CALL 1-800-366-7788 (USA)
or 1-416-499-4615 (CANADA)

CONTENTS

GENERAL INTRODUCTION

by Dallas Willard

The SPIRITUAL FORMATION LINE presents discipleship to Jesus Christ as the greatest opportunity individual human beings have in life and the only hope corporate mankind has of solving its insurmountable problems.

It affirms the unity of the present-day Christian with those who walked beside Jesus during His incarnation. To be His disciple then was to be with Him, to learn to be like Him. It was to be His student or apprentice in kingdom living. His disciples heard what He said and observed what He did. Then, under His direction, they simply began to say and do the same things. They did so imperfectly but progressively. As He taught, "Everyone who is fully trained will be like his teacher" (Luke 6:40).

Today it is the same, except now it is the resurrected Lord who walks throughout the world. He invites us to place our confidence in Him. Those who rely on Him believe that He knows how to live and will pour His life into us as we "take His yoke . . . and learn from Him, for He is gentle and humble in heart" (Matthew 11:29, emphasis added). To take His yoke means joining Him in His work, making our work His work. To trust Him is to understand that total immersion in what He is doing with our life is the best thing that could ever happen to us.

To "learn from Him" in this total-life immersion is how we "seek first his kingdom and his righteousness" (Matthew 6:33). The outcome is that we increasingly are able to do all things, speaking or acting as if Christ were doing them (Colossians 3:17). As apprentices of Christ we are not learning how to do some special religious activity, but how to live every moment of our lives from the reality of God's kingdom. I am learning how to live my actual life as Jesus would if He were me.

If I am a plumber, clerk, bank manager, homemaker, elected official, senior citizen, or migrant worker, I am in "full-time" Christian service no less than someone who earns his or her living in a specifically religious role. Jesus stands beside me and teaches me in all I do to live in God's world. He shows me how, in every circumstance, to reside in His Word and thus be a genuine apprentice of His—His disciple indeed. This enables me to find the reality of God's world everywhere I may be, and thereby to escape from enslavement to sin and evil (John 8:31-32). We become able to do what we know to be good and right, even when it is humanly impossible. Our lives and words become constant testimony of the reality of God.

A plumber facing a difficult plumbing job must know how to integrate it into the kingdom of God as much as someone attempting to win another to Christ or preparing a lesson for a congregation. Until we are clear on this, we will have missed Jesus' connection between life and God and will automatically exclude most of our everyday lives from the domain of faith and discipleship. Jesus lived most of His life on earth as a blue-collar worker, someone we might describe today as an "independent contractor." In His vocation He practiced everything He later taught about life in the kingdom.

The "words" of Jesus I primarily reside in are those recorded in the New Testament Gospels. In His presence, I learn the goodness of His instructions and how to carry them out. It is not a matter of meriting life from above, but of receiving that life concretely in my circumstances. Grace, we must learn, is opposed to earning, not to effort.

For example, I move away from using derogatory language against others, calling them twits, jerks, or idiots (Matthew 5:22), and increasingly mesh with the respect and endearment for persons that naturally flows from God's way. This in turn transforms all of my dealings with others into tenderness and makes the usual coldness and brutality of human relations, which lays a natural foundation for abuse and murder, simply unthinkable.

Of course, the "learning of Him" is meant to occur in the context of His people. They are the ones He commissioned to make disciples, surround them in the reality of the triune name, and teach them to do "everything I have commanded you" (Matthew 28:20). But the disciples we make are His disciples, never ours. We are His apprentices along with them. If we are a little farther along the way, we can only echo the apostle Paul: "Follow my example, as I follow the example of Christ" (1 Corinthians 11:1).

It is a primary task of Christian ministry today, and of those who write for this line of books, to reestablish Christ as a living teacher in the midst of His people. He has been removed by various historical developments: assigned the role of mere sacrifice for sin or social prophet and martyr. But where there is no teacher, there can be no students or disciples.

If we cannot be His students, we have no way to learn to exist always and everywhere within the riches and power of His Word. We can only flounder along as if we were on our own so far as the actual details of our lives are concerned. That is where multitudes of well-meaning believers find themselves today. But it is not the intent of Him who says, "Come to me . . . and you will find rest for your souls" (Matthew 11:28-29).

Each book in this line is designed to contribute to this renewed vision of Christian spiritual formation and to illuminate what apprenticeship to Jesus Christ means within all the specific dimensions of human existence. The mission of these books is to form the whole person so that the nature of Christ becomes the natural expression of our souls, bodies, and spirits throughout our daily lives.

INTRODUCTION

by David Hazard

True lovers understand the simple art of contemplation as well as anyone. If you have ever been in love, or even in longing, you'll know what this means.

A true lover focuses intensely on the beloved, taking in minute detail–the arc of an eyebrow, a characteristic gesture, and what brings a subtle shift in mood. A true lover enters a state of being in which all senses are acutely alert, interior "walls" of resistance down. The universe opens. Colors are brighter. Music is more beautiful. Suddenly, he feels his own being expanding, those inner boundaries made up of likes and dislikes dissolving . . . because he discovers himself liking–to his amazement–things that never attracted him before, but loving them now because they are what the beloved loves. His goals, once centered in his own small ego-wants, crumble in powder . . . replaced by greater goals centered in the good of the other. He is changing at the core, a bit off-balance . . . elated and yet more solidly grounded than ever.

And so it is that a true lover, absorbed in the contemplation of his beloved, is becoming, literally, a new man. The character and nature of the other have changed him.

It is this interaction that we must carry with us, if we are going to understand contemplative prayer—which has sometimes been called "listening prayer." Otherwise, we may be prone to think of it as something that isn't prayer at all but an attempt to use a new technique—as if prayer were a tool—in our efforts to get God to "speak up" more clearly so we can hear Him, or maybe to like us better, or to give us the list of things we're asking for. (Imagine contemplating your boss, staring google-eyed into his face, studying his likes and dislikes, imitating his traits, laughing at his lame jokes, in order to get a raise. I hope you'll feel what you *should* feel.) Or we may approach contemplation as a dry discipline, a practice that will make us "better Christians"—as opposed to, unfortunately, greater lovers of God and other people.

Contemplative praying, and contemplative lifestyle it will create, is really for those who are ready to quit the small, self-absorbed confines of the "old man" . . . and be made new. And nothing is newer in this world than a man or woman who is alive with God's love.

Jan Johnson has explored contemplative prayer and the contemplative life, which has been known to men and women of faith from ages past. She well understands the biblical foundation, and the Hebrew-Christian practices on which this practice rests. For these reasons, Navpress is pleased to include *When the Soul Listens* in our Spiritual Formation Line.

May the path that is laid out in these pages take you more deeply into the life of a Christian disciple—the life of love that is "hidden with Christ in God."

DAVID HAZARD
Senior Editor, SPIRITUAL FORMATION

SECTION ONE

Beyond Asking

WHEN PRAYER STOPS "WORKING"

I SAT IN MY CAR, HIDDEN BY THE EVENING DARKNESS, FRUSTRATED at the way one man had disrupted the committee meeting I'd just left. (I'll call him "X" because I was so irritated I wanted to X him from the committee.) He demanded to have his way and pushed us all so that our committee became polarized—*us* against X. With every new suggestion he made, we rose up to pounce on it. We were going nowhere, so I was glad when the meeting ended.

Now I was waiting in the car for my son to finish his meeting . . . and I was praying for X. Or what passed for prayer. I was ranting to God, "His negativity is ruining the committee. Change this man!"

Even as those words ricocheted in my mind, something happened. I heard the true attitude behind them: *This guy makes me mad. So, God, You should make him do things my way.* Not for the first time, I saw what a *me*-centered prayer I was capable of offering. I was judging X by how he made *me* feel. Because I was frustrated and angry, I had decided on the best course of action. *I* was telling God how to execute my plan. *Wow,* I caught my breath. *Who do I think I am—judging this man, then telling God what to do?*

I let out my frustration with a sigh and shut my eyes. I needed to still my own thoughts and get quiet. I laid my hands in my lap and relaxed my hunched shoulders. A bit of the tension evaporated. I knew I needed to offer a different kind of prayer—selfless, not bossy.

I took a few deep breaths and opened my hands, palms upward in front of me. *He is Yours, God. I leave Him to You.* Breathing more calmly, I allowed quietness to come over my soul and repeated those familiar words: "Be still, and know that I am God" (Psalm 46:10).

I inhaled deeply, praying, *More of Jesus.* And I let that breath go: *Less of me.* My blood was no longer pounding. The evening air felt renewing. Much calmer, I was grateful for the companionship of God and the chance to ponder God's will for X. (The idea that God might have a positive plan for X was still quite a stretch for me.)

For several years I'd been practicing this sort of contemplative prayer—the kind in which you sit before God, simply enjoying His presence. In the heat and pressure of daily living, it's so easy to forget God's presence and slide back into old self-centered habits. But how satisfying to be able to return to this ancient practice, used by Christians for two millennia. I could sense order being restored and peace coming back to my soul. Instead of the unsteady, vengeful feelings that had filled me, I sensed a holy quiet.

AN ANCIENT PRACTICE

For many years of my Christian life, my prayers had been filled with what I wanted. Nothing in my evangelical Christian training had taught me about this quiet sort of prayer—even though the early Christians, church fathers, and saints through the ages, both great and unknown, have practiced contemplation.

Contemplative prayer, in its simplest form, is prayer in which you still your thoughts and emotions and focus on God Himself. This puts you in a better state to be aware of God's presence, and it makes you better able to hear God's voice correcting, guiding, and directing you. Instead of coming with a "to do" list for God, you come with no agenda. The fundamental idea is simply to enjoy the companionship of God, stilling your own thoughts so you can listen should God choose to speak. For this reason, contemplative prayer is sometimes referred to as "the prayer of silence."

As I learned to pray this way, I discovered I *liked* prayer! If I was frustrated, distracted, or confused, I could reconnect with God. There I could find peace and strength. Instead of being stuck in a limited perspective about a person or situation, I would find myself open to a higher view that allowed me to *respond* with patient wisdom instead of *react* out of my emotions.

Eventually, I understood why the inner transformation took place. I would begin my time of contemplation focused on my desires, demands, and needs, saying, *I want*. But by fixing my mind's eye on the God who loved me, something changed. I let go of people, circumstances, myself, and my feelings, and was freed to fix my attention on eternal things. Soon I found myself saying, *God, knowing You is enough for me*.

The change was amazing. I sensed the "peace that passes understanding" which had usually eluded me.

GOD AND MR. X

As calm and order returned on that evening of my committee meeting, I put forth a question to God in the quiet: *What do I need to know about X?*

When I ask God questions this way, ideas sometimes come to me. Other times nothing new comes, but the sense of being reconnected with God is more than enough for me.

In a moment, a favorite breath prayer came to me: "Show me this person's heart." (I couldn't resist adding, "if he has one.") For a few silent minutes, I relaxed and let that prayer rest inside me.

Just then, my son Jeff hopped into the car and said he needed to stop at the drugstore. As we drove, I brought up X's name. Jeff mentioned that X had told stories of fighting in Vietnam. "He said he'd felt helpless, with no control over his life," Jeff filled in. "Sometimes he had to obey orders that he hated obeying." When Jeff walked into the drugstore, I was left alone with God again. I remembered how this man was also laid off from a large firm where he'd been head of the computer department. I thought of his son, too—a great kid, but not cooperative.

Closing my eyes, I asked God again: *What do I need to know?* In the stillness, I saw something I hadn't considered before. *This guy had lost control of so many things—his past, his career, his son.* Did that explain why he was so obviously determined to control things now, including the committee?

Jeff returned to the car, and by the time we got home, a compromise to the committee's dilemma had come to me: *Give him a small portion of the project to control and let the committee run the rest of it.* I called the chair, who liked the idea. In the end, it worked out to everyone's satisfaction. Sometime later, I also realized I had not only experienced peace but, as a result, had been a *peacemaker*—by accident. This intrigued me because my usual method of operation (being a second-born) is *not* to bring peaceful resolution, but to throw dust in the air so I could get away with something I want. (I think this came from messing up my older sister's room and then having to throw the adults off my trail: "Oh . . . her stuff's messed up? Could one of her friends have done it?") I have always marveled at those who can calmly resolve conflict. I've tried to be a peacemaker but failed. This time I'd actually *forged peace!*

What mattered more to me, though, was the improved condition of my heart. I'd become interested in doing what God wanted instead of simply complaining. I no longer wanted to turn the other way when I saw this man, as I'd often done. In future meetings, I felt compassion for him because I had seen his heart. It was another step in the growth toward Christlikeness that I have wanted.

WHEN THE SOUL NEEDS TO BE RESTORED

Over and over, I experience this sort of challenge, correction, and empowerment from God. To a great extent, it has grown out of the practice of contemplation. It involved a major shift—from constantly asking God to change and fix my world to resting in His presence and allowing Him to reshape me from within.

This has been a slow transition for me. I'd been taught many methods of prayer, but most of them involved promoting my agenda. For many years as a Christian, I never sought God *just for God Himself.* Surrendering my old habits of yammering away at God has not come easily. But as I've experienced the peace of God's company, I've found myself turning to "the prayer of silence" as often as possible—even in small snatches of time, as I did in my car that night. Now I wonder how I could have managed my life without it.

Why have Christians regarded contemplative prayer as such an invaluable part of their lives for centuries? One of Jesus' greatest promises was this: "I am with you always" (Matthew 28:20), but we may not experience this. Instead, we keep praying, "God, be with us." That's because we're distracted by life's thousand demands and by our habit of filling in empty time slots with entertainment. Our mind flashes from one thing to another, always occupied. A weekly visit to church can't begin to penetrate this busyness. Contemplation reconnects us with God in the midst of this scatteredness. Life pulls me in so many directions—between the demands of my work, my husband's plans, the kids' needs, commitments outside our home, dreams I want to pursue. . . . I may say I'm "thirsty for God as the deer is for water," but at the moment I need to get my hair cut. However, when I pause to contemplate and be with God, I sense that this God who holds the universe together can also hold me together. In the quiet, I recall how God has helped me in the past. Without the clamor of demands around me, I remember that I am one God *so loves.*

As I experienced contemplative prayer more and more, I sensed a compelling hunger for God and to spend more unstructured time pondering the heart of God. So I decided to make a habit of attending monthly one-day retreats sponsored by a retreat center several towns away. During the third one, I cut out of the sessions early. Outdoors, I climbed down a steep bank that led to a creek running through the property. Stepping on stones, I made my way out to the middle of the flowing water to sit on a huge rock. I didn't say or think anything. It was enough to sit in the sun, listening to the rushing water and lifting my face to God. I didn't have to *do* anything. The only thing required was to *be* . . . and to enjoy the attention of the only One who could give living water to my soul. It seemed like the best place in the world to be.

In between retreats, my days became cluttered with work projects to complete, a household to run, teenagers needing rides to their many events. I longed for those retreat days. I longed to experience a *gatheredness of being* on that rock in the middle of the stream.

As I dressed on the morning of the next retreat, I put on shoes that would help me maneuver the climb and clothes I didn't mind getting snagged by thorn bushes. No matter how interesting the retreat leader would be, I'd skip out to "soak" in the presence of God. Making the ninety-minute drive was a physical manifestation of my spiritual task. Leaving behind my mental trappings (escaping home and work), I was free to trek (the steep path down to the stream) to a place of *collectedness* (the silence and stability of the rock in the rushing creek).

MEETING THE NEEDS OF THE SOUL

When I've talked about having moments of solitude and silence, a few people have eyed me skeptically. Wasn't I talking about "escapism" or having some sort of "mystical" experience?

Contemplation is not an escape from the world or trying to reach lofty spiritual states. Rather, it is a way to face the needs of the hungry soul through simply *being with* God.

The following story illustrates the dynamic of contemplation well: An old peasant went every day into the village church and knelt in prayer. When asked what was wrong and what would make him do such a thing, he said, "I just look at God and God looks at me."[1] He wasn't escaping or searching for ecstasy, just enjoying the presence of God.

The simple practice of contemplation creates a bond with God in which God can heal the scatteredness of our lives and these other unhealthy spiritual states you may be experiencing as well.

Spiritual dryness. My friend Don reflects on "the good old days" of the university fellowship group he attended while in college. In their Bible studies, he and other college students marveled at God's truths, and on weekends they helped each other move. It wasn't unusual for them to take up collections for whoever needed money. No matter where Don goes to church now, he is never moved as he was in those days.

"I wouldn't even know where to begin now," Don says. "My faith isn't gone, but it's been a long time since I've seen God anywhere. I can't even say I want to obey God. I wish I did . . . " In his words I hear a dry, withered soul asking, "Has God my rock forgotten me?" (Psalm 42:9).

To sit in silence before God restores the soul. We don't expect tingly feelings but recollect God as revealed in scriptural truths: God never leaves us, God knocks at our heart's door, God's limitless love and direction is always available. God does not change even though our circumstances do.

When our soul is dry, contemplation connects us with the One who "is eternal [so] His love can have no end; because He is infinite, it has no limit; because He is holy, it is the quintessence of all spotless purity; because He is immense, His love is an incomprehensibly vast, bottomless, shoreless sea before which we kneel in joyful silence."[2] His love waters our thirsty soul.

Guilt and shame. Our unfinished business with God disturbs us within and won't leave us alone. Recurring sins don't go away. Feelings of inadequacy never end. Lack of purity plagues us. These things make us afraid to face God in prayer. Who wants to see a disapproving look on the face of God? Uneasy questions drive us away from God: *Shouldn't I feel ashamed of asking God's forgiveness over and over for the same sin? Is God tired of me? Is there hope for me? When will all these sermons click and I'll finally stop snapping at my kids or yelling at other drivers on the road?*

In contemplation I envision myself as the lost sheep whom the Shepherd has come to find (see Luke 15:1-7). I ask these questions as the Shepherd carries me home on his shoulders: *I've been found, but am I still welcome? Am I still included in the fold? Am I still a vessel God can use?* I'm reassured to be sitting on the shoulders of a Shepherd who's planning to throw a party for this bumbling sheep (see Luke 15:6).

Lack of direction and purpose. When I'm not fitting in or understanding what's going on around me, I need to hear the directing voice of the Father.

A. W. Tozer, one of the most influential evangelists of our century, wrote, "Most of us go through life praying a little, planning a little, jockeying for position, hoping but never quite certain of anything, and always secretly afraid that we will miss the way."[3] In uncertain times, I want to trust God that my life will count, that God will use me, weak as I am. I become more uncertain as I see the skills, opportunities, success, and faith others have—and I begin to compare myself and my circumstances, until I'm telling myself, *I can't . . .* and *I don't have . . .*

A few minutes of quiet with God allow me to soak in the biblical truth that I am one God *so loves,* possessing "a hope and a future" (see John 3:16, Jeremiah 29:11). As I absorb God's truthful words, my doubts and fears are challenged. A sense of trust develops. In the quiet I can rest in God, who knows what's going on even when I do not. When we're stuck in these inner currents, a heart relationship with God does not seem possible. We feel disconnected. But when our soul listens, we can regain sight of God as the One who is eager to nurture us and get us up and walking again.

SHIFTING THE FOCUS

At the root of these problems of disconnectedness is the fact that my spiritual life is about me and what I want. It is not centered upon God and what God wants. We understand prayer to be mostly about asking God for things, and when God doesn't seem to answer, we are wounded, disappointed, and eventually hardened toward God. Why didn't God play fair?

Once, at a retreat, a woman complained to her discussion group that if she had known I would mention prayer so often, she would not have come. She'd prayed for a depressed friend and for her seriously ill mother. The friend committed suicide and her mother didn't get well. "What good has prayer ever done?" she asked the group. Many people feel this way — Why bother? —but they never verbalize it as honestly as this woman did. She had goals about fixing and mending her broken world, and in her eyes it seemed God was not interested in her goals. Therefore, for her, God didn't work.

How do you view God? The way you understand God, and the way you understand how God works, matters.

I used to view God as something like a magic genie, responsible for cleaning up life's messes and keeping the pantry full. At other times, I viewed God as a giant aspirin to relieve my aches and pains. In essence, I reduced God to a servant or a vending machine. I put my coin of faith (prayer) into the slot and expected to find the prize (happiness, achievement, success) in the tray at the bottom.

Yet I never saw that my prayer was based only on my thoughts and desires. I put myself in the center of things and said, *This is what seems right and good to me, so it must be the best thing. And now,*

God, I want it. Use your power to make this happen. I was proud of my twentysome-page prayer request list—which amounted to a spiritualized "to do" list for God. Yes, I praised and thanked God. But then I began giving God orders: Change this man! Now would be the preferred time for You to do this!

WHO CONTROLS YOUR LIFE?

Underneath it all, the heart vies for position with God, turning good spiritual teachings to its own advantage. For example, I used to love phrases like "Prayer is the key that unlocks the storehouses of God's riches." I was hungry for those riches and imagined I could use prayer to get them. I missed the point—the riches are God Himself, not the goodies I want God to provide. Turn-of-the-century writer Evelyn Underhill pinpointed the problem: "We mostly spend [our] lives conjugating three verbs: to *want,* to *have,* and to *do.* Craving, clutching and fussing, we are kept in perpetual unrest."[4] My jabbering prayers have been full of what I *want,* what I think I should *have,* and what I want God to *do.*

It's no surprise that these demanding prayers go unanswered. Then the legalistic voice inside begins to say, *God is ignoring your prayers because you're not good enough.* If we're eager or desperate enough to pursue prayer, we intensify our efforts toward God, resulting in practices like these:

Formula praying. We work hard to find the "correct method" to persuade God, constantly searching for new formulas for prayer. We get excited over new and better techniques, gadgets, or systems to increase the effectiveness of prayers.

Devotion to the tools. We talk about "believing in prayer," indicating how much we put our faith in our prayers and their "power." (I no longer *believe in prayer;* I believe in God alone. Prayer is a vivid, varied place—a state of my soul—in which I connect with God.)

You may think that differentiating between devotion to God and devotion to spiritual tools is a small thing, but this important issue caused Jesus to be at odds with the Pharisees. The sect of the Pharisees focused on spiritual practices, such as ceremonial washing and rigid Sabbath-keeping. They looked down on Jesus because He did not. Jesus focused on God Himself. This frustrated and angered the Pharisees because they used "spiritual tools" to gain God's favor— and here was Jesus ignoring their formulas and gyrations, focusing on the love of God, and speaking about God with such confidence.

Focusing on the "tools" of our faith is a sign of self-absorption: *Have I prayed today? Did I pray long enough, sincerely enough for it to "count" with God?* With all good intentions, we can become navel-gazers, focusing on our efforts. Oswald Chambers, author of the classic work *My Utmost for His Highest,* says, "Beware of being obsessed with consistency instead of being devoted to God."[5] When I eyeball my own performance too closely, my spirituality is about *me,* not about God.

Pastor Peter Lord, author of *Hearing God,* challenges us to test ourselves with this question:

> If God gave you nothing but himself, would you be satis-
> fied? The answer reveals whether you love God for
> himself, or for what you hope He will do for you. When
> you find yourself no longer enjoying the presence of God,
> when you find your prayers are limited to asking for things
> for yourself, you are in a hurry to get answers for your
> needs, when Christian ministry becomes the all-important
> thing in your life, then there is the subtle danger that you
> are using God for your ends.[6]

In the end, it comes down to this: Either we are struggling to control our own lives—or we are learning to rest in God and take our cues from Him.

INTO THE HEART OF GOD

I've introduced you to a kind of prayer that waits silently, focused on God and asking nothing. Yes, it's true that asking is also part of the Christian life. Jesus asked the Father for many things (see, for example, John 17).

First and foremost, however, prayer is about *aligning ourselves with the will of a powerful, loving God,* not using "the right phrases" to persuade, cajole, or manipulate God. This is not an employee-boss relationship, in which we never know when we'll be terminated, and so seek to get as much out of the boss as we can while we still have a chance. The spirit of Christian prayer is the attitude of *surrendering ourselves to be vessels of His good purposes.*

When we continue to use prayer to ask for things, something happens inside. Our faith is reduced, as author Flannery O'Connor put it, to little more than "an electric blanket."[7] We pull it out hoping God will cover the cold, exposed spots of our lives. That's all. God listens and smiles . . . but will not become our divine genie. And we become disillusioned with God. Imagining He has let us down, we become estranged from Him. In a culture that teaches us to perform for rewards, prayer becomes one more place of defeat and God is one more disappointment. We may even keep going through the motions spiritually — going to church, helping others — but in our heart we wonder, *If God is good, wouldn't He give me the good things I want? Because He doesn't, either God is not good, or I'm hopeless.*

We come to a dismal place because we misunderstand prayer as a means to have our desires fulfilled instead of a place to encounter the compassionate, all-seeking God. As we understand prayer correctly, we move from devotion to the *tools* to devotion to the *Master.* This difference is described well in the following analogy by Tony Campolo:

> There are two ways that I can tell you how to get from [wherever you are] to Eastern College where I teach. I can give you a map that charts out the route for you to take. With such a map you might or might not get there, depending on how good you are at reading maps [and whether roads are closed]. The other option I can offer is to get into your car, sit beside you, and direct you as we go along.[8]

Are you a map reader or a companion of God? Learning to converse with God — sharing my true hurts and sensing the heartbeat of God — is so much better than being devoted to prayer as a formula. God created us not to make us map-reading, rote followers, but to have a love relationship with Him. No one's voice or opinion is more important than the voice of the One who loves us most and best. Jesus told us, "[The Spirit of truth] lives with you and will be in you" (John 14:17), as well as "I am in my Father, and you are in me, and I am in you" (John 14: 20). Even when we have strayed as the nation of Judah did, we can count on God's constant, loving guidance: "Whether you turn to the right or to the left, your ears will hear a voice behind you, saying, 'This is the way; walk in it'" (Isaiah 30:21).

CONNECTING WITH THE GOD WHO LOVES YOU

One of the settings in which your ears are likely to "hear a voice behind you" is in contemplation because it's about being with God, the lover of your soul. "The point of prayer," Oswald Chambers affirms, "is not to get answers from God, but to have oneness with Him. If we pray only because we want answers, we will become irritated and angry with God."[9] Picture a child constantly asking a parent for things. This badgering not only annoys the parent, but the poor child is miserable. We can be children of God who love God for who He is — not for what He gives us — and experience an end to our dryness and disillusionment.

When being with God counts, we no longer come up with clever plans and then ask God to give us the strength and know-how to accomplish this course of action we've already chosen. Prayer becomes a meeting of the hearts as I rest in God's presence. Finding a good plan is not my chief goal, but rather living in the company of God is.

The purpose of this writing is to help you learn how to meet with God in life-transforming encounters in which your heart comes to rest in His presence. As we explore contemplative prayer together, expect God to invade all of your life. As you become more focused on His presence, you will find yourself conversing with God throughout the day. This is because the silence and solitude practiced in contemplation creates an interior quiet and calm that permeates mundane activities.

This living from the heart of God teaches you to see people as Jesus saw people. For example, while riding in the back seat of my car, my friend Liz saw some boys wearing handcuffs in the car next to us. I saw them too, and my first thought was, *Uh oh. What did these guys do?* But Liz said, "I should pray for these boys. I wonder what's going on in their lives." This is how prayer becomes the main business of your life.[10] You don't go for hours in forgetfulness of God and God's work on the earth. Even when you have nothing important to say to God, you are satisfied being with Him—coming and going, working and resting.

REWARDS OF GOD-CENTERED PRAYER

When prayer is a place to delight in God, we find ourselves hungry for God. We imitate Jesus, running off for solitude: "At daybreak Jesus went out to a solitary place" (Luke 4:42). Imagine Jesus momentarily leaving His mission and the demands of the crowds to set out into the barely light, still-damp out of doors—after an exhausting day of driving out demons and healing people. Why didn't He sleep in? It would seem that Jesus longed for God. Parents of preschoolers know this longing for adult conversation. At night you tuck your children in bed, feeling just a little bit of relief because now you can converse with your spouse without interruptions.

Contemplative prayer opens us to a conversation with One we love, and so prayer becomes something we *like* to do. Like jet-skiing, reading a detective novel, or visiting an old friend, you don't have to gear up for it by trying hard to think "God thoughts" for a few minutes. We become completely, authentically ourselves with God—with no need to impress.

And God becomes real in us.

Have you been longing for depth and authenticity with God? Do you need the renewing power of God in you? Do you want purpose and daily direction? In the course of this book we will explore the methods and benefits of contemplative prayer, which opens us up to the wonder of God's presence. If prayer has stopped "working" for you, if you want to know the reality of God, I invite you now to explore contemplative prayer and the lifestyle that allows you to experience God's presence. This sense of God's presence will also change you (something we will explore in the next chapter) and give life and empowerment to your soul.

Isn't that what you've been wanting?

NOTES

1. Avery Brooke, "What Is Contemplation?" *Weavings*, July/August 1992, p. 7.

2. A. W. Tozer, *The Knowledge of the Holy* (San Francisco: HarperSanFrancisco, 1961), p. 98.

3. Tozer, p. 63.

4. *Great Devotional Classics: Selections from the Writings of Evelyn Underhill*, ed. Douglas Steere (Nashville, TN: The Upper Room, 1961), p. 10.

5. Oswald Chambers, *My Utmost for His Highest: An Updated Edition in Today's Language*, ed. James Reimann (Grand Rapids, MI: Discovery House Publications, 1992), November 14 entry.

6. Peter Lord, *Hearing God* (Grand Rapids, MI: Baker, 1988), pp. 194-195.

7. Letter to Louise Abbot as recorded in *O'Connor Collected Works* (The Library of America, 1988), p. 1110.

8. Tony Campolo, *How to Be Pentecostal without Speaking in Tongues* (Dallas, TX: Word, 1991), p. 65.

9. Chambers, August 6 entry.

10. Richard Foster, *Celebration of Discipline* (San Francisco: Harper & Row, 1988), p. 34.

A NEW YOU

FOR MANY YEARS, I WORKED HARD TO BE SOME KIND OF A decent Christian. Nothing worked. Selfishness, grouchiness, and laziness dogged me. Prayer and serving God were duties. And when I did something right, I became self-satisfied, certain that I'd discovered what you and ten million other people *had* to know. So I'd tell you.

As I've laid down my hardworking attempts to be "some kind of decent Christian," I've discovered a subtler means of change. By quietly centering on God—not myself—that transformation has begun to occur. Not only do I *like* praying and long to do so, but God has also used it as a means to change my soul, my personality, my desires.

BOB AND ME

I have volunteered for some time at a local drop-in center for the homeless. My job entails keeping a list of clients who have signed up for showers, and letting them know when it's their turn. As I stood behind the counter one day, Bob[1] peered at the shower list I'd put together and asked, "Shouldn't I be going in now?" I looked up into his face. One eye was missing, and that side of his face was badly scarred. I smiled and showed him how far down on the list his name still was.

Then with a look of meanness I'd never seen before, he leaned across the counter and growled, "If you know what's good for you, you'll move me up on the list!"

Surprised, I asked, "Are you threatening me, Bob?"

Bob swaggered back a few steps and stared at me with his one good eye, not sure of what to make of my challenge. I wasn't sure what would happen next. Then he turned and walked out.

A few minutes later the director, who'd heard about the incident, came to ask if I was going to quit.

"No," I said. "My goal here is not to be popular. Mostly, I come here to pray. Lately, I've prayed a lot for Bob."

When Bob had come to our church a few weeks before, my friend recognized him. She worked at the grade school he had attended years ago and where, she said, "He became more and more troublesome in the developmentally disabled class until he dropped out. It was later that he crawled into the sewer drain and shot himself."

I blinked hard when she said that. *Bob had lost his eye trying to commit suicide?* I'd assumed it happened when he was drunk and in the wrong place at the wrong time. I'd been thinking about that when I was praying for him that morning at the center.

The next time I volunteered, Bob came and put his arm around my shoulder. "How's Miss Jan today?" he said, glaring at me. I wondered if he was testing me, asking in his own way, *Will you—you little religious person, you—still be my friend?* I smiled and talked with Bob, praying for him silently as I often do when we talk. I sensed my welcoming response was a small but important piece of evidence that God loved him no matter what.

Every personality test I've taken rates me as "nervous" and "fearful." But the *me* who volunteers at the drop-in center is quiet and attentive. That's because I'm praying as I work. Rarely do I use words. When I do, it may be only one word, such as "peace" or "comfort" or "courage." When I do this, my awareness of God's presence affects me to the point that I behave with love when normally I would not. If only I could live this way all the moments of my life!

A DIFFERENT AGENDA

Back in the days when I tried so hard to be a "decent Christian," I would not have lasted long as a volunteer at the center. I would have asked God to reform Bob, and if that request didn't "work" (Bob didn't get a job or find a place to live), I would have burned out on him. By being patient and nice, I would have attempted to get him to respond in kind. His threatening behavior would have meant I was a failure, so it would have been time to quit.

Learning to focus on God has changed my agenda-driven approach to folks like Bob. The sense that I'm not here to change the world, but only to pray and partner with God in His work, has come from the new sense of interior rest I have found in adopting a contemplative style of living. It's made a world of difference, giving me a sense of commitment to guys like Bob even when I see no immediate "fruit."

Yet *I am not saying I've finally found the "secret" to getting my prayers answered.* Not at all—in fact, that's no longer the issue. More and more, the issue is *knowing God Himself, and learning to perceive and follow God in all His ways.* My spiritual life is more about God and what God does, less about me and my strivings.

THE HEART OF THE MATTER

The life that God asks from us is simple. It consists of loving God and paying attention to God, and in so doing, we sense His mind and heart. We sense our role in God's plan and start to live out of the heart of God. God communicates His blessings to others through us. In a slow but definite way, we experience a "change of heart." As Glenn Hinson, professor of spirituality at Baptist Theological Seminary, says, "A change of heart is the heart of the matter."[2]

This openness to God and the subsequent transformation of our heart brings a holiness, compassion, and courage that seemed unattainable before. To do this is to see the spirit of Jesus Christ formed in us—a process long known to Christians as "spiritual formation," in which the character of Christ is fashioned in us.

Spiritual formation is using certain practices to cultivate an inner life that is strongly connected to God. This inward life results in the transformation of our outward behavior. Through this process, we become disciples of Jesus Christ imitating both His inward heart attitudes and His outward behavior. In this way we become, in Paul's words, "clothed" with Christ (see Galatians 3:27), exhibiting Jesus' radical humility, mercy, and courage. One of the ways we get this wrong in our Christian teaching is by addressing outward behavior only, without paying attention to the condition of the heart. Rather than working to bring change from the inside out, we focus on outer appearances. For example, we correct a child for not saying "thank you" for a gift or favor without finding out what's going on inside him or her. It's more important to us that the child *appear* thankful so we spare ourselves embarrassment for the child's lack of social graces. That act of saying "thank you" becomes more important than cultivating in the child a thankful heart.

God, however, emphasizes the importance of the inner being and the changes He means to forge there. Jesus said, "The kingdom of God is *within you*" (Luke 17:21, italics mine). The apostle Paul spoke of the Word of God being "at work *in you* who believe" (1 Thessalonians 2:13, italics mine). He also focused our attention on "God who works *in you* to will and to act according to his good purpose" (Philippians 2:13, italics mine). Although outward acts matter (you can tell the type and health of a tree "by its fruit," Matthew 7:20), God looks first upon the heart (see 1 Chronicles 28:9, Psalm 119:10, Jeremiah 29:13).

Our efforts at "spiritual growth" are more often attempts at changing outer behavior. Christians of other eras understood that our growth comes from cooperating with God as He works to form a new spirit in us. Spiritual formation pays careful attention to the soul, using spiritual practices that open us to God's work there. As David said, "You teach me wisdom *in the inmost place*" (Psalm 51:6, italics mine). And Paul prayed, asking that God "may strengthen you with power through his Spirit *in your inner being*" (Ephesians 3:16, italics mine).

CONTEMPLATIVE PRAYER AND SPIRITUAL FORMATION

Contemplative prayer is one of the practices that gives God time and access to work in our inner person, changing the attitudes of the heart that ultimately drive us. A changed heart (Matthew 7:17) can't help but produce "good things out of the good stored up in his heart." Conversely, a person who is not inwardly good cannot produce good things (see Luke 6:43,45). The task, then, is to let God make us inwardly good, to have a heart full of love—then our outward behavior will change.

The consequence of focusing on external behavior while ignoring the inner person is enormous. Lack of attention to the soul produces a person who can be rooted in godly desires, maybe even religious organizations, but whose heart is numb to God. The Pharisees were the most pious of the pious, the religious conservatives, and the keepers of the Book in Jesus' day. Yet Jesus railed at them in an attempt to crack their self-righteous shells. The Pharisees did things many of us would love to have to our credit: They were admired and respected for being like Moses (see Matthew 23:2). They were honored at public events (see 23:6) and recognized in the streets as great spiritual people (see 23:7). They witnessed (see 23:15); understood fine intricacies of spiritual correctness (see 23:16); knew well the facts of Israel's history (see 23:30); tithed (see 23:23); and discerned right from wrong in their culture (see 23:16-18).

How can people do so many things right and still get it so wrong? The pharisaical heart is acquired by doing things admired in religious culture but *not letting God reshape the heart*. Jesus' assessment of those spectacular religious achievers of His day was this: Yes, they look beautiful on the outside and appear righteous (see 23:27,28), but they are full of greed and self-indulgence, hypocrisy and wickedness; they are dead and corrupt on the inside (see 23:25,27,28). They lacked justice, compassion, and faithfulness (see 23:23). The outward things that we do for God mean little if they have not sprung from a heart that is intertwined with God's justice and compassion. In the end, you cannot do the work of Christ without the heart of Christ.

FOLLOWING JESUS

To have our heart reshaped in the image of Christ is critical. In fact, this process of spiritual formation was understood for centuries to be the normative path for *all* those who claimed to follow Jesus, not just certain mature ones. Yet the process of reshaping the heart is little known in some branches of the church today. In recent years, we've paid more attention to upholding correct doctrine or using God as a problem solver. It seems we've lost the bigger picture of the road to discipleship—growing in the character of Jesus Christ. Instead, we seem to believe that if we hear enough Bible facts or inspirational sermons, we're bound to change somehow.[3] When that doesn't do the job, we reinvent ourselves with self-help books and quick tips from talk radio. God can use these things as pieces of our puzzle, but improving our lives a bit here and there is not the same thing as being a disciple of Jesus.

This lack of understanding of spiritual formation makes the Christian life a bumpy and unstable walk for many believers. We need to be pumped up with heart-tugging stories or shamed with statistics of how pathetically unspiritual we are. We must be spoon-fed by the church or wind up leaving because we're "not being fed." When sermons don't grab our attention or the worship music no longer excites, we move on.

To insist that the church take responsibility for all the care and feeding of my soul is to be a "consumer Christian." Is it someone else's task to connect me with God—or is there a living, breathing God at the door of my heart waiting for me to invite Him inside for a chat? Don't I have a responsibility to help myself be nurtured by God? Nothing can create our spiritual life for us—not the sermon, not the worship service, not a daily devotional guide, not the next book by a favorite author. God calls me to be discipled by Christ. My job is to sit before God in quiet contemplation and say, "Show me the next step."

We can cooperate with God in our spiritual formation by cultivating an awareness of God and an openness to His direction. Then we can follow His lead as Jesus did, not trying to lead God as we usually do. That is humility; that is what it means to be "clothed" with Christ. As we find our life centered in God, problems such as scatteredness, spiritual dryness, overriding shame, and lack of guidance fade.

As the heart of Christ is formed in us, our behavior automatically changes. We no longer see the "Mr. Xs" as irritating enemies, but as souls that God loves and directs us to love. By my surrendering Mr. X to God, God brought peace to my soul as I became a vessel of His love to a combative person (for a few minutes, anyway). (I also found out later that I provided a better example to my son by loving instead of complaining and backbiting.) That's what will always happen as our inner person is trained to follow Jesus.

TRAINING THE SOUL

So how does spiritual formation occur? Growth in Christlikeness occurs as we use certain accepted practices described in the Bible and practiced by Jesus. Just as a future concert pianist uses techniques and practices to train herself for the intended goal, a believer can benefit greatly from the practice of "spiritual disciplines."

These disciplines, so overlooked today, create back-and-forth contact with God—allowing God to transform our character and personality to resemble His own. In this book we will address the discipline of contemplative prayer in its various forms: listening prayer; wordless contemplation; waiting on God; and practicing God's presence.

Contemplation is only one of many spiritual disciplines that help us grow in the character of Christ. In general, disciplines help us *engage in* or *abstain from* certain practices in order to track with the mind of God. Through the ages, these became known as disciplines of *engagement* and *abstinence.* Disciplines of engagement include things such as study, worship, prayer, celebration, service, fellowship or community, confession, and submission. The disciplines of abstinence help train the soul by requiring us to keep away from activities or substances. These disciplines include solitude, silence, fasting (for example, from eating food, watching television, or spending money), frugality, chastity, secrecy, and sacrifice.[4] Indeed, it has been said that a spiritual discipline is anything that helps you practice "how to become attentive to that small voice and willing to respond when we hear it."[5] These are ways to interact with the Spirit of God so that the Spirit moves in your heart in the depths of personality far beyond the conscious mind, intentions, and thoughts.

Some Christians balk at the idea of spiritual disciplines. They equate them with good works aimed at "earning" salvation. But we are not talking about earning favor with God. In and of themselves, spiritual disciplines have no merit. If we do them to earn favor with

God or other people, they are self-righteous works and we eventually burn out or become hardened legalists because "the letter kills, but the Spirit gives life" (2 Corinthians 3:6). But if we practice the disciplines in order to connect with God, they become vehicles through which God can change our behavior. When they are used to bond with God, spiritual disciplines retrain the heart, tongue, feet, lips, arms, and knees. (See 1 Peter 3:10, 2 Corinthians 10:5, James 4:8, Ephesians 6:15, Colossians 3:8, Hebrews 12:12.) This results in the spiritual formation of soul and body. Take for example the spiritual discipline of prayer. It may be done for selfish purposes, as we've seen, or to connect us with the heart of God. Oswald Chambers considered the famous adage "Prayer changes things" and realized it was an incomplete and misleading statement. He rephrased it, saying, "Prayer changes *me* and I change things." He elaborated, saying, "Prayer is not a matter of changing things externally, but one of working *miracles* in a person's inner nature."[6] Those interior miracles Chambers talks about occur in the process of spiritual formation. You gradually change from being a person who pushes your own agenda to a person who listens to others. You no longer need to be right, but you want to do the right thing. You become reshaped from TV values ("You can never be too rich, too thin, or own too flashy a car") to the values of God's kingdom—justice, mercy, and faithfulness.

Consider the spiritual discipline of *Bible study* as another example. Do we study the Bible to have our soul conformed to the image of Christ? Or if we fail to read the Bible, do we think, *No wonder things are going wrong—I didn't do my Bible study, so now God isn't blessing me.*

When you delve into Scripture to know the heart of God, the discipline takes on life and becomes satisfying to the soul. You no longer worry about getting to the bottom of the page or finishing the chapter if God has spoken to you in the first verse. This word may cut so deep that you need to use other disciplines —you stop and *meditate* on it to taste and see it. (You may even meditate on the same passage several days in a row, allowing God to continue to show you more.) Then it may help to *journal*, committing your soul to paper. Capturing new insights on paper gives them substance and adds strength to the impulse to change. The next day you may want to sit in *silent contemplation,* resting before God to see if more insight comes to you. As God's voice becomes more clear, you may talk about it with a friend, using the discipline of *fellowship* or *community* to keep this matter from slipping back into the darkness, unconfessed and undealt with.

Finally, as you act on the new light you've been given, you *serve God* as a changed creature and experience the truth of God's Word. Any spiritual discipline involves hearing God's voice in some way.

A TRANSFORMED CHARACTER

As we are transformed, we no longer work hard to do good things good people are supposed to do. We put our effort into simple disciplines that connect us to God. And that effort results in more faith, knowledge, self-control, patience, godliness, brotherly love, and *agape* love (see 2 Peter 1:5 and following verses). Good baseball players train behind the scenes by practicing their batting day after day, with no crowds watching.[7] When they step up to the plate in the spotlight, the swing is automatic and steady. Connecting with God through disciplines such as contemplative prayer allows God to train us "behind the scenes" to know, hear, and follow Him. Then in the spotlight of troublesome situations, we are less likely to "slip" with rude outbursts because the soul has been submerged in the love of Christ behind the scenes in private.

The effort put forth in a spiritual discipline is not to change behavior, but to connect our inner person's motives and needs with God. The effect of that connection is a change of heart.

As I have practiced God's presence (a form of contemplation) while I drive, my driving attitudes and behaviors have changed. In my early years of driving, I deserved many more speeding tickets than I got. When I received my first one, I yelled at the police officer and made obnoxious comments. When I got another one ten years ago, I'd begun practicing the presence of God as I drove—praying for people I passed. My heart had changed enough that I knew I deserved the ticket and said nothing. After that, I was far more diligent about driving the speed limit and watching for pedestrians.

A few months ago, hurrying to the high school to get my son to a doctor's appointment, I was caught again. As soon as I saw the flashing lights of the patrol car, I cried in repentance. Every morning for years I'd enjoyed practicing God's presence as I'd driven my kids to school, praying for the kids in the neighborhood I drove through. How could I endanger these people I'd prayed for so often? Love is *slowly* changing my motivations, convincing me that my reason for hurriedness is never more important than the person standing a few feet from me. Now I want to obey speeding laws, not just to avoid the inconvenience of a ticket, but because I know Christ cares for the people around me and He's persuaded me to do the same.

This change of heart is at the core of spiritual formation: We are transformed into vessels of God's love. We are caught up in a new and renewing exchange of intimacy with God, who is Love, which allows God to change our character and personality. Prayer involves less asking and becomes more like sitting as the clay in the Potter's hand, receptive to God's molding and shaping. The more you love God, the more you obey Him—by loving others, behaving with integrity, giving sacrificially. The more you obey God, the more you love God. Love begets obedience, which begets love until they become the same thing.[8]

This natural obedience, motivated by a changed heart of love, is much different from trying to be good or doing good deeds. For example, I can try hard to be kind to the "dragon lady" on our block—but I'll want credit for any little progress and I'll give it up if she doesn't change. If, however, I pray for her when we talk, looking at her through the eyes of Christ, I will unconsciously be more considerate and attentive to her. During our conversation, I will have interacted as much with God as with her. Living this way, with your soul open to God while you are present to others, has a transforming effect. God's love lives in you and changes the way you behave. This is why Madame Guyon could insist, "The only genuine means of bringing about change is by inward means."[9]

This results in doing the work of Christ with the heart of Christ. This is a "righteousness which exceeds that of scribes and Pharisees" (Matthew 5:20). This true righteousness is about bending our knees to the Father, rending our hearts in repentance and exposing our souls to God, so His voice can simmer in our heart. Only with this heart of Christ can we effectively do the work of Christ, which may result someday in being "some kind of a decent Christian."

NOTES
1. Not his real name.
2. E. Glenn Hinson, "Horizontal Persons," *Weavings*, March/April 1995, p. 23.
3. "The Door Interview: Dallas Willard," *The Wittenberg Door*, June 1993, Issue 129.
4. I modified this list from Dallas Willard, *The Spirit of the Disciplines* (San Francisco: Harper & Row, 1988), p. 158.
5. Henri Nouwen, *Making All Things New* (San Francisco: HarperSanFrancisco, 1981), p. 66.
6. Oswald Chambers, *My Utmost for His Highest: An Updated Edition in Today's Language*, ed. James Reimann (Grand Rapids, MI: Discovery House Publications, 1992), August 28 entry, second italics mine.
7. This comparison originated from and is expanded in Willard, *The Spirit of the Disciplines*, p. 3.
8. I didn't see this relationship between love and obedience until I closely examined John 14:15-24 . The words "love" and "obey" each occur three times. What is their relationship? To love is to obey (verses 15,23); to not obey is to not love (verse 24). "For virtue, is nothing else than an ordered and controlled affection which has God for its single object, himself alone. For he himself is the pure cause of all the virtues." *The Cloud of Unknowing*, Fr. James Walsh (Rahwey, NJ: Paulist Press, 1981), p. 147.
9. Madame Guyon, *Experiencing God through Prayer*, ed. Donna Arthur (Springdale, PA: Whitaker House, 1984), p. 38.

"MY SHEEP HEAR MY VOICE"

I SAT QUIETLY BEFORE GOD WITH THE INVITATION IN MY HAND. After years of hard work and yearning, I'd been asked to spend the weekend with a group of journalists who are considered elite in a field in which I longed to be a "star." It would mean networking and career advancement otherwise not possible and hobnobbing with some of the "greats."

But . . . I already had a speaking engagement on the same day. True, it was eight months away and I could call the event planner—an acquaintance—and cancel. This was perhaps the reasonable thing to do. Except for the image that kept coming back to me—one that made me open my eyes from my contemplation and lay the invitation down.

About a week before, I'd spent time meditating on the passage in which Jesus said: "Make every effort to enter through the narrow door, because many, I tell you, will try to enter and will not be able to" (Luke 13:24). As I'd pictured myself walking through the narrow door with Jesus, I knew that my narrow door had a sign over it that said *Integrity*. For years, I'd fumed about the lack of integrity I saw in other Christians, and God seemed to be calling me to walk through that "narrow door" of integrity myself. What's more, in my meditation, God had assured me that the door of integrity is not grievous but pleasant. It would be a walk with Him, after all, and He said: "People will come from east and west and north and south, and will take their places at the feast in the kingdom" (verse 29). Feasts are fun, aren't they? So integrity couldn't be as painful as I imagined it to be.

So I slid the invitation back into the envelope, knowing I would not change my plans. I was disappointed, but at the same time, I wasn't. I had a great desire to walk through the narrow door. I wanted to enjoy the feast of God.

Months later, when I reflected on this, I saw that the miracle was not just that I behaved with integrity, but that I did it without a sinking heart. The day of the event I was glad to be there. In the past, I'd done a lot of right things while harboring poor attitudes. For once, I was doing the right thing with a full heart. I tell this story so that you'll see how contemplative prayer is rooted in Scripture. I was able to "hear" God in contemplation about keeping my engagement because I had already "heard" God through a Scripture passage I'd meditated on. There God had shown me that integrity is not so painful and had drawn me to want to live that way.

The Bible is full of examples of men and women who listened, rested, waited, and conversed with God. To people of faith, the contemplative interchange with God was not uncommon. When we think of examples of prayer in Scripture, we tend to remember the spectacular stories of fleeces and partings of waters, pleading and plaguing, imploring and importuning. We tend to overlook the many instances of resting and waiting in order to clear the mind and listen. Because we forget these, you may be wondering, *Is contemplative prayer safe? Is it biblical? I've never read the words "contemplative prayer" in Scripture—what does Scripture say about it?*

Scripture commands us to listen over and over. Wise men and women of Scripture are characterized by their "abiding" in God—a deep-heart listening to God. Let's look at the details.

LISTENING TO THE GOD WHO SPEAKS

Jesus said that His followers listen to the Shepherd's voice (His) and train themselves to recognize it easily. They know how to follow (obey) because they know His voice:

"The sheep *listen to his voice*. He calls his own sheep by name and leads them out. When he has brought out all his own, he goes on ahead of them, and his sheep follow him because they *know his voice*. But they will never follow a stranger; in fact, they will run away from him because they *do not recognize a stranger's voice*. My sheep *listen to my voice*; I know them, and they follow me." (John 10:3-5,27, italics mine)

Yet most of us prefer listening to a pastor or speaker rather than training ourselves to sit in quiet and listen to God. We are in good company. God desired to speak to the Israelites until they put their foot down and insisted on hearing only from Moses (see Exodus 20:19). Oswald Chambers writes:

We show how little love we have for God by preferring to listen to His servants rather than to Him. We like to listen to personal testimonies, but we don't want God Himself to speak to us. Why are we so terrified for God to speak to us? Perhaps it's because we know that when God speaks we know we have only two choices: Either we will do what He asks, or tell Him we will not obey. But if it is simply one of God's servants speaking to us, we feel obedience is optional, not imperative.[1]

Throughout the Bible God addresses this issue of learning to hear Him at least twenty-four times,[2] offering both invitations and warnings: Those with hearing ears who accept what God says are the ones who become partners with Him in the work of His kingdom (see Matthew 11:15, Mark 4:9, Luke 14:35); those who refuse to listen are in danger because their hearts are "callused"—that is, covered up with a thick layer of fleshly concerns so the sensitivities of the spirit are dulled (see Matthew 13:13-15). Jesus emphasized the importance of having the eyes and ears of the soul trained upon God.

Scripture is clear that we can develop "eyes to see" and "ears to hear." And yet . . . contemplation doesn't come naturally. Many mornings I wake up and the chatter begins in my head—words to say, work to do, and places to go. I'm not listening to God at all. I have to stop and pray, many times borrowing these words of John Baillie:

> O God, give me grace today to recognize the stirrings of Thy Spirit within my soul and to listen most attentively to all that Thou hast to say to me. Let not the noises of the world ever so confuse me that I cannot hear Thee speak.[3]

As the "sheep of God's pasture," we seem to move through different stages of knowing God's voice and recognizing His movements, and it may be helpful to understand these stages:

We fail to recognize God. As a boy, the prophet Samuel kept running to Eli the priest, saying, "Here I am; you called me." God had been calling to Samuel, but the young boy mistook it for the voice of his mentor. As we begin our life of seeking God, we need someone to help us recognize when God is stirring our soul, someone to send us back to silent, waiting prayer, where we can say to God, "Speak, for your servant is listening" (1 Samuel 3:5,10).

We recognize that God has been leading, nudging . . . but after the fact. Jacob awakened from dreamy sleep, thinking, "Surely the LORD is in this place, and I was not aware of it" (Genesis 28:16). We are like the bewildered folk of yesteryear who said of the Lone Ranger, "Who was that masked man?" We're slow, but we do get it eventually.

We recognize God's presence and voice immediately. Elijah could listen to the commanding noise of wind, earthquake, and fire—but he was trained enough in the ways of God to recognize God's voice in a gentle whisper (see 1 Kings 19:11-13).

Learning to understand God and His movements is not a terrible challenge but a wonderful path of discovery. As Oswald Chambers writes:

> The attitude of a child of God should always be, "Speak for Your servant hears." If I have not developed and nurtured this *devotion of hearing*, I can only hear God's voice at certain times. At other times I become deaf to Him because my attention is to other things—things which I think I must do. This is not living the life of a child of God.

Chambers finished this confession with this stunning question: "Have you heard God's voice today?"[4]

As we take seriously Scripture's command to listen to and recognize God's voice, we face a challenge: Either we remain in charge of our lives, following the voice of our natural inclinations—or we resign as the planner and designer, producer and director of our own life . . . and surrender ourselves to God daily.

For me, this means stepping out of myself, reflecting silently in the company of God, and asking questions like these:

- Am I aiming to be one with You, Father—or do I only come to You to have my needs met?
- Am I longing for soul growth or to have others think well of me?
- Am I trying to push my plan on You, God—or do I want to let You show me your plan?

RESTING AND WAITING

Scripture's primary prayer book, the Psalms, also emphasizes the fine art of resting and waiting on God, which along with listening, is part of contemplative prayer. One psalmist spoke to his own soul about rest, saying: "Find *rest*, O my soul, in God alone; my hope comes from him"; "Be at *rest* once more, O my soul, for the LORD has been good to you" (Psalm 62:5, 116:7, italics mine).

Rest is demonstrated by the outward silence of contemplative prayer. To be quiet and vulnerable before God is a concrete form of laying all in God's hands and not worrying about who I am and how I'm perceived. The shadow of the Almighty is a great place to *rest* for the soul that is scattered, parched, guilt-ridden, or uncertain (see Psalm 62:1,5; 91:1; 116:7). Quiet rest allows God to speak to your deepest self, and so David instructs: "When you are on your beds, search your hearts and be silent" (Psalm 4:4). Resting and reflecting on the God encountered in Scripture is encouraged in Psalms and Habakkuk with the word *selah,* which occurs seventy-four times. Though it is often dismissed as a mere musical notation, most commentators agree that *selah* was inserted at points where the singer or psalm reader should pause so listeners could reflect.[5]

Waiting on God is an honorable pastime in Scripture, even though it's not popular in our typical life in the fast lane. We talk about "being in God's waiting room" as if it's worse than any medical waiting room in existence. But Scripture shows how waiting, a long-practiced way of praying, doesn't have to be boring, but can be full of alert, expectant peacefulness: "I *wait* for the LORD, my soul *waits*, and in his word I put my hope" (Psalm 130:5, italics mine). The expectancy is electric as described by Wisdom (the figure in Proverbs who many commentators understand to be Jesus) saying: "Blessed is the man who *listens* to me, watching daily at my doors, *waiting* at my doorway" (8:34, italics mine).

John the Baptist, the ascetic wilderness dweller, described the outcome of being a waiting and listening friend to God: "The friend who attends the bridegroom waits and listens for him, and is full of joy when he hears the bridegroom's voice. That joy is mine, and it is now complete" (John 3:29).

CONVERSING WITH THE ALMIGHTY
Out of resting, waiting, and listening springs genuine conversation with God. Consider how naturally whole conversations between Abraham and God developed out of the interior calm of resting, waiting, and listening:

- God stated the covenant and appeared to reassure Abraham (see Genesis 12:1-7). God reminded Abraham of the covenant promise when Abraham was cheated by his relative and business partner, Lot (see Genesis 13:14-17).
- God again spoke through the priest, Melchizedek, to affirm that Abraham was headed in the right direction (see Genesis 14:18-20).
- Abraham presented God with the bleak picture of the future, in which the covenant failed due to infertility, and God reassured Abraham of the covenant with a visual aid, a dream (see Genesis 15:1-21).
- God went over the covenant again. Abraham bargained for an Ishmael clause, but God declined and expounded on the original proposal (see Genesis 17:1-22).

- God appeared and spoke through three strangers. God reviewed the covenant again and stated His one-year plan (see Genesis 18:1-19).
- God and Abraham discussed Ishmael as a threat to the covenant (see Genesis 21:8-13).

Many other covenant-related events occurred in Abraham's life, but this list represents the spoken words between God and Abraham (at least the ones we know about). We wonder if Abraham should have had even more discussions with God because he ended up hurting the people he loved when he acted without these discussions with God (offering his wife to foreign rulers twice; agreeing to the Hagar-as-surrogate-mother scheme). History provides us with a picture of God speaking to people—and they're better off for it. Some people might object to the idea of having conversations with God. Why talk? Just obey! Between God and Abraham, shouldn't it have been, "God said it, Abraham believed it, that settled it"? But the point of resting, waiting, and listening is to build relationship. And Abraham's continuing "conversation" with God deepened that relationship, as conversation over years of time deepens a human relationship. God went so far as to call His relationship with Abraham a "friendship" (see 2 Chronicles 20:7, Isaiah 41:8, James 2:23) because Abraham not only listened, but he also acted upon God's voice.

The truth is, resting, waiting, and listening are states of the soul that we can carry with us anywhere. In fact, what fascinates me are the ordinary, and often busy, settings in which God spoke with people. An angel, representing God, appeared to Gideon in an ordinary workplace—a winepress, a pit in which strenuous labor went on (see Judges 6:11-12). When Jesus appeared and spoke with His disciples after the Resurrection, He met them as He did everyday tasks—walking on roads and cooking at the beach. We often equate God's speaking to us with having a bright-light experience like Paul did on the road to Damascus (see Acts 9), but the more frequent experience is to find God speaking in the ordinary, even hectic, places of life. To me, this underscores the importance of having "ears to hear" throughout our day, especially in the midst of mundane activities.

FAILING TO RECOGNIZE THE VOICE OF GOD

If God is this interested in speaking to us, why do we fail to perceive His voice? Here are the two most common reasons.

Many believe God no longer speaks to us today. Some Christians insist that two-way exchanges with the Father no longer occur. They believe that anything the Bible says about listening to God or the guidance of the Holy Spirit applied only to a certain time in history.

True, God does speak to us through the recall of Scripture. But is God's voice limited to this avenue only? That would mean God no longer convicts our hearts personally. Instead, our spiritual convictions are mere mechanical activity of the skilled intellectual mind. "Hearing" God is available only to Christians brainy and clever enough to remember Bible passages word for word and able to apply them with finesse. Regarding the puzzlements of life, has God left us alone to figure them out for ourselves? Does God no longer speak to the heart, but guide us only through words on a page? Does God supply no specific ideas of how you and I can love opponents, accomplish justice, welcome the stranger, or disciple a newcomer? Must I be wise enough to discover what obedience to God looks like in each situation without help from Him?

Usually, those who insist God no longer speaks to individuals, giving personal guidance, also insist we can have a "personal relationship with God." How can I have a personal relationship with God if I'm the only one who talks? How can it be "personal" if I can never have a private audience with God? Or perhaps God may hear me personally, but God doesn't respond to me personally. Conversation with God is vital to a personal relationship.

To believe God only speaks in and through recalled Scripture verses cuts short the work of the Holy Spirit. We do wrong to "think of God as mute everywhere else and vocal only in a book," wrote A. W. Tozer. He insisted it is shortsighted indeed to live as if "a silent God suddenly began to speak in a book and when the book was finished lapsed back into silence again forever. Now we read the book as the record of what God said when He was for a brief time in a speaking mood. The facts are that God is not silent, has never been silent. It is the nature of God to speak."[6]

Perhaps this idea—that God is with us but silent—is an over-reaction to the wild claims people have made over the years, predicting the end of the world, the end of paper money, and the end of cellulite. These claims are appalling, but they emphasize how important it is to be trained to hear the voice of God with clarity—especially contrasted with the voice of one's ego. (We will discuss more about pitfalls in chapter 10.)

The antidote to wild-eyed prophets is not to reject the notion that God speaks, but to be trained in hearing Him well. This gets at the subtle relationship between Scripture and contemplative prayer.

Contemplative prayer requires an accurate knowledge of the God of Scripture. There is a strong correlation between a working knowledge of the Bible and learning to hear His voice leading us in our lives. That is because a head knowledge about God from the Bible becomes a heart knowledge of Him as we practice contemplative prayer. If the head knowledge is wrong, the heart knowledge will be also.

We fail to know what Scripture teaches of God. We sometimes fail to recognize God's voice because we don't have an accurate head knowledge of who God is in Scripture. Therefore, when we pray and seek God, the inaccuracies we believe take over.

Perhaps we see God as a tyrannical creature who pulls the rug out from under us, sabotaging our dreams. Or one whose favorite activity is criticizing and condemning when He's not dreaming up earthquakes and tornadoes. Perhaps He sleeps a lot and wakens only to pat us on the head. These images of God don't reflect a Father who likes us very much. He gets tired of our mistakes and constantly raises His eyebrows and mops His forehead, hoping we will shape up so He can move on to the people who really matter.

True, if you were to ask most Christians, they would tell you, "God is love." But stick around. It won't be long before they speak of how "God must be fed up with me now." This is not just a problem for new or immature Christians. Every few weeks, I hear the following phrase from even the most mature of Christians, male and female: "God slapped me up side of the head this week." When I mention this in my retreat talks, it's not unusual for someone to gasp because they'd heard it in the last week.

We have imposed on God mean-spirited characteristics that resemble the capricious and vengeful Greek gods and goddesses rather than the Jehovah of Scripture. It is not unusual, for example, to hear jokes about God's use of lightning bolts to correct people, but this is not scriptural. According to Scripture, no one was ever struck by lightning. (Of the forty-six times lightning is mentioned in Scripture, it's used as a metaphor for quickness and to describe the majesty of God. Only once during the plague of the hailstorm in Egypt does it strike the ground in punishment.) I wonder, do we turn God's majesty into terror on a regular basis? Is the truth of what we believe in our hearts revealed in our humor? *The truth about God's character is found in the whole of Scripture.* To know the Bible well is to hold a broad and balanced understanding of both God and His ways with us. As Peter Lord writes, for example:

> [God] will correct your behavior, but he never condemns your worth. It is the enemy who sends all such thoughts as "I am no good," "I will never amount to anything," "I am a failure," "I am a nobody," "I am not important." But God says you are his "dear one" (he chose you and knows all about you), his "beloved child," and a thousand other wonderful things.[7]

Even as God speaks to you about your soul's neediness, He does so not to shame you but for the healthy formation of your character.

Why do we need a full, healthy picture of God?

LOVING GOD . . . AND LIKING HIM

Before contemplative prayer can become something we *want* to do, we must understand God as someone we *want* to be with. Our natural reaction is to avoid prayer if we don't really know who God is: "Yes, I see my faults in contemplative prayer, but I'm not being beaten up by God." We can drench ourselves in the images of God we find in Scripture:

- *Friend*: "Abraham believed God, and he was called God's friend" (James 2:23).
- *Forgiving father*: See the father running down the trail to

embrace the prodigal son; forgiving the sanctimonious older son by saying, "You are always with me. Everything I have is yours" (Luke 15:20,31).

- *Tender mother*: Note the tenderness of the parent feeding the child and teaching the child to walk (see Hosea 11:1-4).
- *Spouse of our soul*: In Hosea's story, Hosea represents God and his wife, Gomer, represents Israel. I see in this passage God and me. I "chase" after "lovers"—self-importance, controlling others, self-gratification—while God keeps coming up with different, wily ways to pursue me—walling me in with a hedge of thorns, leading me to a lovely vineyard (see Hosea 1–3).
- *Sole lifelong companion*: "The LORD himself goes before you and will be with you; he will never leave you nor forsake you. Do not be afraid; do not be discouraged" (Deuteronomy 31:8, see also John 14:18).
- *Captain of our salvation*: "For it became him, for whom are all things, and by whom are all things, in bringing many sons unto glory, to make the captain of their salvation perfect through sufferings" (Hebrews 2:10, KJV).
- *Overly generous boss*: The master paid a full day's wage to unemployables who weren't hired until the last minute (see Matthew 20:1-16).

We take in these scriptural images and, as Paul Jones says, we can trust that:

God's love is the promise never to treat us with an eye for an eye. God's unconditional intention is to turn the other cheek, walk the second trillion miles, and forgive seventy light-years times seven—dressing us all the while with a royal cloak to cover our stolen coat.[8]

If we are to enjoy contemplative prayer, we must know and love the God of the Bible. Elijah, who was so skilled at recognizing God's voice and who conversed with Him regularly, also knew firsthand the loving heart of God. Afraid and running for his life, he asked God to take his life. Instead of chastising Elijah for this self-destructive request, God set up a routine for him to sleep and then eat food from the hands of angels. Well-acquainted with God's tender mercies, this austere prophet was hungry to hear God speak in the wilderness silences where he was forced to dwell.

You and I dwell in a wilderness of silences, too. It doesn't look like a wilderness because it's full of people and buildings—but it is a spiritual wilderness just the same. And all around us we hear the incessant noise of televisions, traffic, radios, and machines. It drowns the voice of God's Spirit into silence—if we let it.

Believers down through the ages have found ways to "leave behind" the wilderness of the world to seek the living presence of God in contemplation. Their example and their words can help guide us on this new path. It is to their wisdom we now turn.

NOTES
1. Oswald Chambers, *My Utmost for His Highest: An Updated Edition in Today's Language*, ed. James Reimann (Grand Rapids, MI: Discovery House Publications, 1992), February 12 entry.
2. Deuteronomy 29:4; Psalms 115:6; 135:17; Proverbs 20:12; Isaiah 6:10; 30:21; 32:3; 42:20; Jeremiah 5:21; 6:10; 9:20; Ezekiel 12:2; 40:4; Matthew 11:15; 13:9,15-16,43; Mark 4:9,23; 8:18; Luke 8:8; 14:35; Acts 28:27; Romans 11:8.
3. John Baillie, *A Diary of Private Prayer* (New York: Collier Books, 1977), p. 73.
4. Chambers, February 13 entry, italics mine.
5. H. C. Leupold, *Exposition on Psalms* (Grand Rapids, MI: Baker, 1972), p. 61.
6. A. W. Tozer, *The Pursuit of God* (Camp Hill, PA: Christian Publications, Inc., 1982), pp. 81-82.
7. Peter Lord, *Hearing God* (Grand Rapids, MI: Baker, 1988), p. 132.
8. W. Paul Jones, "Love as Intrinsic Living," *Weavings*, January/February 1998, p. 28.

CHAPTER 4

A CLOUD
OF WITNESSES

As WE SAW IN THE PREVIOUS CHAPTER, CONTEMPLATION IS ROOTED in Scripture. Yet it is not widely practiced in some Christian traditions today—most notably, the evangelical and Pentecostal traditions.

You may be wondering, Who are the Christians who have practiced contemplative prayer? What did they learn about life in Christ and knowing God? How can I be sure this isn't a fad—an influence of the New Age or a leftover from the Maharashi's Eastern mystical influence?

Contemplation is well known within the larger context of the history of our faith. It is, in fact, rooted in two thousand years of Christian experience. Throughout the ages, mature believers who spent significant time praying in this silent way have written about it. Beginning with early church fathers such as Augustine of Hippo, later with Bernard of Clairvaux, and down through the ages in the anonymous work *The Cloud of Unknowing*, the contemplation of God has been a central topic among His people. Devotional masters such as Teresa of Avila, John of the Cross, Brother Lawrence, Madame Guyon, and Jean-Nicholas Grou recorded timeless insights into seeking the heart of God. Their works are considered spiritual classics.

Describing the contemplation of God, Bernard of Clairvaux (a twelfth-century abbot and founder of more than sixty monasteries) wrote of an "inward paradise of pleasure [where] vision of pure truth illuminates the eye of the heart (Ephesians 1:18). The most sweet voice of the inner Comforter brings joy and gladness to the ears."[1] Contemplation has long been a place of gazing at God in great delight.

The classic texts from such saints are important because they offer us not only wisdom and insight but structure and safeguards as we enter contemplation. First, they make it clear that contemplation is rooted in the study and meditation of Scripture. Classic writings about the contemplation of God are full of references to Scripture, as if the writers had taken their cues from God's text. As a result, the rootedness in Scripture keeps contemplation from becoming a way to put words in God's mouth.

Second, Christians of the past saw contemplation as firmly rooted in the context of discipleship and spiritual formation—that is, the Christian's need for growth in the character of Christ (which we discussed in chapter 2). Bernard of Clairvaux wrote:

[During contemplation], a foretaste of the incomparable delights of love is enjoyed, and the mind, anointed with mercy and freed from the sharp thorns and briars by which it was once pricked (Isaiah 10:17), rests happily with a clear conscience (Acts 23:1; 1 Timothy 1:5).[2]

Therefore, quiet moments of contemplation were not seen as "tingly experiences of rapture," and certainly not moments when God "elevated" someone to a higher plane than other believers. In fact, contemplation brings us down to earth very fast because it causes us to see ourselves as we really are.

Rooted in Scripture

Contemplation isn't based on empty-headedness or airy fantasies, but on the foundation of study, reflection, and prayer—so wrote the fourteenth-century author of *The Cloud of Unknowing*. Those "who do not make the effort to ponder God's Word should not be surprised if they are unable to pray [contemplatively]," wrote this anonymous

English man or woman.[3] Thomas Merton, a twentieth-century Trappist monk, concurred. Contemplation is "embedded in a life of psalmody, liturgical celebration and the meditative reading of Scripture (*lectio divina*)."[4]

What is *lectio divina?* *Lectio divina* is a classic method of Scripture reading which includes contemplative prayer. Pronounced lex-ee-oh di-vee-nuh[5] (which is Latin for "divine reading"), it has been used widely among believers, especially in Benedictine monasteries, beginning in the sixth century.[6] Contemplation falls fourth and last in the *lectio* format:

- Reading a Scripture passage (*lectio*)
- Meditation on that passage (*meditatio*)
- Prayer (*oratio*)
- Contemplation (*contemplatio*)

If the wordless, agendaless aspect of contemplation troubles you, notice how countless Christians through the ages have practiced it within the structure of Bible reading, meditation, and prayer. Contemplation always begins from a bedrock of Scripture. This is one significant difference between Christian contemplation and other forms (we will consider other differences in a moment).

Before *lectio* participants pray contemplatively, they read the Bible and pray, which are familiar activities to contemplative believers. They also meditate (the second phase), which may be less familiar to many of us.

Meditation, a process of prayerfully pondering words and events of Scripture, was commanded and practiced throughout the Bible (see Genesis 24:63; Joshua 1:8; Psalm 1:2; 19:14; 39:3; 48:9; 77:12; 104:34; 119:15,23,27,48,78,97,99,148; 143:5; 145:5). Meditation invites you to settle in a verse or passage, finding words and images in which you can nest and rest. You insert yourself into the text, thereby letting it insert itself into your heart.

TRAINING THE SOUL

But how do you meditate? You and I meditate every day as we consider how to land a better job or redecorate a room. In fact, if we know how to worry, we know how to meditate. When we worry, we ask, "What if (this terrible thing) happens?" And we rehash all the awful possibilities. When we meditate, we focus on a Scripture and ask, "What if I had been the person Jesus healed? What would that experience have been like?" Entering the text this way retrains the soul by helping us encounter God in a personal way and live in the sense that we have been spoken to personally by God. The stunning result of these encounters with God is that our natural tendencies to be self-centered are overridden by the desire to please the God we have just encountered.

So meditation is different from Bible study. In Bible study, we dissect the text; with meditation, we enter into the text. When studying, we ask questions about the text; in meditation, we let the text ask questions of us.[7] After studying a passage in which Jesus miraculously heals and making sure we understand the implications of the Greek verb tenses as well as the culture of that day, we go on to ask, "What would it be like to be touched by Jesus the way He touched this person? To have Him put His fingers in my ears and touch my tongue so that His hands cradle my cheekbones as He did the deaf and barely speaking man? (See Mark 7:33.) To have Him grasp my hand and feel the heat leave me and energy pour in so that I can instantly get up and do what I've been unable to do? (See Matthew 8:14-15.)"

Studying a Bible passage can prepare us to meditate on it, but then we must shift gears. Henri Nouwen, a priest who left a prestigious position at an Ivy League school to become spiritual director at a community for handicapped adults, wrote:

> Instead of taking the words apart, we should bring them together in our innermost being; instead of wondering if we agree or disagree, we should wonder which words are directly spoken to us and connect directly with our most personal story. We should be willing to let [the words] penetrate in to the most hidden corners of our heart, even to those places where no other word has yet found entrance. Only then can we really "hear and understand" (Matthew 13:23).[8]

How Meditation Builds a Base for Contemplation

Just as study and reading prepares us to meditate on Scripture, meditation prepares us to contemplate. When we meditate, the focus is on the words and images of the passage, while contemplation focuses us on resting in God.[9] Meditation helps us savor the truth about God, and contemplation makes it sweet to our soul. In contemplation, words are less important than fellowship with the Father. As Avery Brooke observes, "Meditation investigates, contemplation wonders."[10]

The early writers set the example for fixing our contemplative gaze on God. Augustine, a fourth-century bishop in the Mediterranean seaport of Hippo (now Annaba, Algeria), spoke of "He who fills heaven and earth (Jeremiah 23:24) without being limited by finite space . . . nowhere absent. . . . He is completely present everywhere, but contained in no place."[11]

The task for us, then, is to fix the eye of our soul upon the greatness of God. As you meditate on Isaiah 6:1-8, for example, you picture the high and exalted throne and the six-winged seraphs singing (this can be difficult to picture because we're used to two-winged angels). You feel the shaking of the doorposts and smell the smoke filling the room. (At first, this scene reminded me of a dazzling Amy Grant concert, but in further study I learned that because this was the temple, the smoke came from incense and sacrifices.) So as you gaze on this scene, you can enjoy the fragrant smells of incense mixed with waves of backyard barbecue aromas. You see Isaiah speaking and the seraph touching his mouth with the coal. Finally you hear Jesus speak (see John 12:41). He addresses someone, perhaps the heavenly hosts, saying, "Who will go for us?" Isaiah jumps into the conversation and volunteers to be the one to go. Like Isaiah, you are humbled, cleansed, and ready to serve. You see how microscopic you are in the scheme of things in the universe. You are awed by the God you worship and His willingness to include you in His plan.

Add to this scene the possibility of sitting in awe of the character of God. Augustine referred to this as the ability to "perceive the beauty of God. For we normally think of perceiving beauty with our eyes, but the beauty of God is in His complete goodness—consisting of virtues or high truths that are all of His nature. These high truths—love, holiness, faithfulness and the like—we may look upon only in the depths of our soul."[12]

After you have meditated on this passage, it is time to contemplate this scene, wordlessly absorbing the transcendence of God. In this way, contemplation is a "gee whiz!" response to meditation. It opens the soul to view the heart of God. You may naturally be moved to ask, "God, what are You saying to me through this?" But it's important to remain truly fixed on God Himself, not on seeking an answer, so you remind yourself that you are simply posing a question. An answer, if needed, may come . . . tomorrow . . . or next year. True contemplation has no agenda other than learning to rest in God.

The more we meditate and contemplate, the more God permeates the ordinary moments of life. Inexplicably, Augustine tells us, we "hold on to a constant inner vision of Him,"[13] even in unlikely places. At odd moments, the majestic, high truth vision of God comes back to me so that while sitting with my friend at her son's soccer game, I long for "the world to come, [when] those who are to receive the kingdom prepared from the beginning for them (Matthew 25:34), all the clean of heart, shall see Him."[14]

But is all this possible—even wise—in this world where our feet are planted firmly on the ground? Yes, wrote Bernard of Clairvaux:

> The contemplation of God is not a reward of eternal life,
> but the "wages of the soldiering of this life. [T]hey do not
> belong to what is promised to the Church in the future, but
> rather to what she is promised now."[15]

Considering how bleak this side of heaven can be, I'm so glad for the contemplation of our God, who doesn't shrink from showing His graciousness in the midst of family squabbles and contract disputes—if that "inner vision" is trained on Him.

In my early experiences of contemplation, I saw the wisdom of the classic contemplatives who rooted contemplation in biblical study and meditation. My husband had been laid off and I was just beginning to receive income as a writer. I felt nervous about our financial state. One day, as I sat in silence waiting on God, a terrifying picture erupted in my mind: I was shipwrecked and left alone in the ocean. What I was sensing was so vivid that my lips felt pickled from saltwater and my face burnt by the sun. As fear gripped me, however, familiar verses from Psalm 18 flashed in my mind. They told of a person about to die: "The cords of death entangled me; the torrents of destruction overwhelmed me" (verse 4), but God parted the heavens and came down, mounting the cherubim and flying in as dramatic a rescue as John Wayne ever graced the screen with (verses 9-10). Then in my mind I saw God plucking me out of the water: "The valleys of the sea were exposed and the foundations of the earth laid bare at your rebuke, O LORD, at the blast of breath from your nostrils. He reached down from on high and took hold of me; he drew me out of deep waters" (verses 15-16).

The terrifying inner turmoil passed and I recalled that picture many times in the uncertain days ahead.

Some Christians object to meditation because it uses the imagination. It is wiser, however, to give our imagination to God to be retrained by Him than to withhold it. The process of spiritual formation allows every part of our being to be embraced and schooled by God, and the imagination needs retraining as much as anything else. If we ignore our imagination, it finds entertainment of its own. When activated by the images and truths of Scripture, the imagination enables the penetrating Word of God to become active in our lives.

Others are suspicious of meditation and contemplation because they are often practiced in nonChristian world religions. But the fact that others use these God-ordained practices does not ban them for use by those who follow Jesus Christ. Mahatma Gandhi prayed a great deal and frequently quoted Jesus, as does the Dalai Lama today. Yet we do not give up praying or reading the Gospels because these leaders of other faiths practice these disciplines. As believers in Christ, we do not use the techniques of contemplation in the same way that practitioners of Eastern religions use them. Our goals are different. In Eastern religions, the goal of contemplation is to reach a place of nothingness. As Christians, our goal is to empty ourselves by meeting with God and allowing His image, heart, mind, and will to fill us. "For the Easterner the goal is to reach *nirvana*, which means 'where there is no wind'—no disturbance of the soul. For the

Christian, the wind and fire of the Spirit is vital, even when it blows harshly. The Eastern practitioner moves from meditation into contemplation, into self-annihilation, into death, in order to be freed from the 'intolerable wheel of life.' As Christians we move—rather, *we are moved*—into death [to self] in order to be discovered, to be loved into truer life by our Maker."[16]

TOOLS FOR MEDITATION AND CONTEMPLATION

To enter into the experience of meditation and contemplation, it is helpful to understand basic tools God has given us. These are simple things, available to us all:

- *Five senses.* In meditation, we imagine ourselves seeing, smelling, tasting, hearing, and touching the concrete details of the passage. A. W. Tozer pointed out:

  The same terms are used to express the knowledge of God as are used to express knowledge of physical things. "O *taste* and see that the LORD is good" (Psalm 34:8). "All the garments *smell* of myrrh and aloes and cassia, out of ivory palaces" (Psalm 45:8). "My sheep *hear* my voice" (John 10:27). "Blessed are the pure in heart, for they will *see* God" (Matthew 5:8). These are but four of countless such passages from the Word of God. What can all this mean except that we have in our hearts organs by means of which we can know God as certainly as we know material things through our familiar five senses?[17]

- *Images and pictures.* Jesus taught in images, which reach a more affective part of us and can make it easier to obey. Earlier I mentioned meditating on Luke 15:1-7 and gaining a richer understanding by considering the image of Jesus my Shepherd carrying me—the lost, *smelly* sheep—on His shoulders. Scripture teaches me that the Shepherd didn't *yell* at me when He found me. I learn that I am the speechless woman who timidly *touched* the hem of Jesus' garment, *speaking* aloud, telling Jesus the whole truth (see Mark 5). More often, however, I am the rich young ruler who, arrayed with great spirituality, pulls up in front of God in my Jaguar, and then I am confronted by Jesus, who *looks* at me, loves me, and challenges me to release my grip on the things and people I hold most dear (see Mark 10:31).

What images in Scripture are powerful to you? Are you open to being enriched by new ones? Once I was challenged by a retreat leader who said that we often limit our images of God. As I sat by the creek, I knew he was right. I saw God primarily as my protector. I was hiding under His wings (see Psalm 17:8). I was running into His tower and dragging my family along behind (see Psalm 61:3). So I asked God, "What else?"

As I prayed, I sensed that I would always need protective images because fear is such an automatic response in my life. "But what else?" I asked. I opened my eyes and began paging through poetic sections of Scripture, looking for images. In the Psalms, I ran across the words "thunder" and "lightning" several times. I shut my eyes again, and asked, "What does it mean to see You, God, as a lightning bolt in my life—moving me forward, supplying me with electric energy to move?" I looked to make sure no one could see me and then did a set of steps from my exercise workout that somehow had a lightning-bolt feel. What was that about? These movements were in themselves a wordless prayer, as if I were giving God permission to work His great will in my small life. Spiritual formation, as I've noted, retrains not only the mind and heart, but the body as well. That's why so many spiritual disciplines involve actions of the body—confession and celebration, fasting and chastity. God dwells in the whole person.

FOR THE SAKE OF OTHERS

Devotional masters of the past have wisely emphasized that the purpose of the contemplative way is *not* for blessing ourselves or making ourselves happy, but for our spiritual formation.

"Contemplation brings the solid food of wisdom (Hebrews 5:14), made from the finest flour," observed Bernard of Clairvaux.[18] With this wisdom, we are better able to love God, and by loving God to love others (see 1 John 4:11,20-21). This *others-centered* dimension of spirituality is why Asbury Seminary professor Robert Mulholland carefully included in his definition of spiritual formation this phrase: "being formed in the image of Christ *for the sake of others*."[19] God is forming me spiritually so that I am able to partner with Him in reconciling people to Him (see 2 Corinthians 5:18-20).

Contemplation turns our heart inward to sense the work of God in us—and at the same time it turns our heart outward toward others. That is because contemplation equips us to tune in to people rather than tuning them out. It was through contemplation that I saw the heart of Mr. X. When I practice contemplation regularly, I see others differently, so I'm more likely to ask a friend or family member, "What do you think God has been saying to you recently?" rather than "Would you do me a favor?" In rich solitude with God, I drop my annoyance with a nonverbal member of my family and realize that he shows love through action not words. Contemplation detaches us from the stings of our opponents so we can feel the most meager sort of love for them because we see them through the eyes of Christ.

It is this transformed heart and vision that moves us outward. Jesus' encounter with Legion has had this kind of powerful affect on me (see Luke 8:26-39, Mark 5:1-19). In my mind's eye, I've watched Jesus talk to this man possessed by thousands of demons. I've had to turn my head from this homeless, naked man living in a seaside graveyard among the cliffs. I've wondered what he did to be kept under guard, chained hand and foot. I've cringed at the noise level of his crying and the odor of dried blood. I've felt mesmerized by how Jesus walked up to this guy, met his needs, and showed him compassion without being intimidated by the evil of the demons. I've taken these impressions into contemplation and marveled at how God specializes in the throwaways of a culture.

The other day, when I meditated on this passage again, I noticed for the first time that the Gospels don't mention anyone but Jesus getting out of the boat. (In meditation, it's not unusual to open your eyes and check the Bible for details because details feed meditation.) I saw myself as a reluctant disciple staying behind in the boat, eager to make my getaway, so glad my children didn't come on this outing to see this X-rated spectacle of nudity and violence. Yet Jesus, the

Rabbi who had no business talking with this ceremonially unclean Gentile, approached him anyway.

Then I began to contemplate the self-giving, fearless love of Christ, and grieved for the "Legions" on this earth and for myself because in my life I do not get out of the boat enough. I wound up asking God to give me the gift of being a disciple who gets out of the boat more often to love other people with the heart of Christ. I sat there for a long time caught up in the desire to be like Him.

Late that night I dashed to the grocery store with my daughter. As we hurried into the store, preoccupied with our shopping list, I half noticed someone sleeping under the public telephone outside. Just before checking out, I turned to my daughter and asked, "Was that Lana[20] curled up under the public telephone outside?" She said it was.

Lana is one of the neediest clients at the drop-in center where I volunteer. In fact, I've often avoided her outside of stores in "off-duty" moments. That night I went back outside to see what Lana needed before we checked out. I invited her to come with me to pick out food, but she had eaten. She then offered me part of her sandwich. The rest of her words were incoherent. A few of them were in English but not strung together in sentences I could understand. I looked at this twenty-something woman in sweat pants and bedroom slippers and listened to her talk. I tried not to weep, then I hugged her, remembering the likelihood of lice only as I was letting go. Not until I got into the car did I remember Legion. Apparently, my time with God that day changed me enough on the heart and soul level so that I could not ignore Lana. God had melted my heart of stone a little bit more into a heart of flesh, and so I was that much more a vessel of His love and light to her when He needed me to be.

Because times of meditation and contemplation detach us from others, we can see people as God sees them. If I sit quietly before God, imagining you as I pray, it's harder for me to only half listen to you the next time you speak to me. So even though meditation and contemplation are inward experiences, they equip us to behave outwardly with the justice and mercy of Jesus. Because this is part of our spiritual formation, the obedience is so natural it almost seems accidental. And this is good for people like me; then my obedience does not come about because I am centered on myself and trying hard to be Christian, but because I am centered on the nature and character of Christ. This is how, little by little, the character of Christ is formed in us. Now that we have looked at some of the basics of contemplative prayer, in the next section we will turn our attention to grasping the methods of contemplative prayer and how it becomes a way of life.

NOTES

1. *Bernard of Clairvaux: Selected Writings, The Classics of Western Spirituality,* trans. Gillian Evans (New York: Paulist Press, 1987), pp. 84, 85.
2. *Bernard of Clairvaux: Selected Writings,* pp. 84, 85.
3. *The Cloud of Unknowing,* ed. William Johnston (New York: Doubleday, An Image Book, 1973), p. 93.
4. Thomas Merton, *Contemplative Prayer* (New York: Doubleday, An Image Book, 1996), p. 28.
5. Norvene Vest, *Gathered in the Word* (Nashville, TN: Upper Room Books, 1996), p. 11.
6. Vest, p. 126.
7. Jan Johnson, *Listening to God: Using Scripture as a Path to God's Presence* (Colorado Springs, CO: NavPress, 1998), first page of Introduction. More explanation of the differences is provided there as well as more explanation of *lectio divina.* This book also leads you through *lectio divina* style meditation on thirty passages of Scripture.
8. Henri Nouwen, *Reaching Out* (New York: Doubleday, An Image Book, 1975), pp. 135-136.
9. Thelma Hall, *Too Deep for Words: Rediscovering Lectio Divina* (New York: Paulist Press, 1988), p. 9.
10. Avery Brooke, "What *Is* Contemplation?" *Weavings,* July/August 1992, p. 10.
11. *Augustine of Hippo: Selected Writings, The Classics of Western Spirituality,* trans. Mary T. Clark (New York: Paulist Press, 1984), p. 384.
12. *Early Will I Seek You,* ed. David Hazard (Minneapolis, MN: Bethany 1991), p. 77.
13. *Early Will I Seek You,* p. 81.
14. *Augustine of Hippo: Selected Writings,* p. 380.
15. *Bernard of Clairvaux: Selected Writings,* p. 85.
16. Madeleine L'Engle, *Walking on Water: Reflections on Faith and Art* (Wheaton, IL: Harold Shaw Publishers, 1980), p. 194.
17. A. W. Tozer, *The Pursuit of God* (Camp Hill, PA: Christian Publications, Inc., 1982), p. 51.
18. *Bernard of Clairvaux: Selected Writings,* p. 104.
19. M. Robert Mulholland, Jr., *Shaped by the Word* (Nashville, TN: The Upper Room, 1985), p. 27. The last phrase has been added by him since he wrote the book. I was informed of this when I edited a portion of his book for the *Spiritual Formation Bible.*
20. Not her real name.

SECTION TWO

How Contemplation Works

CHAPTER
5

THE
CONTEMPLATIVE WAY

W HEN PAT'S HUSBAND DIED FROM BRAIN CANCER, HER FRIENDS
were eager to help her. One of her friends, Miriam, invited her
to go to "human potential" seminars. Pat didn't like the seminars but
she enjoyed the company of Miriam, who was a Buddhist, so she
went. One night on the way home, Miriam began to speak about
Christ and ask Pat questions about Him. Pat found it interesting
because she had never mentioned her faith. Miriam's interest quickly
deepened and she accepted Christ, as did her husband, Kiet. Pat continued to go to seminars with Miriam, and during breaks, Miriam's
Vietnamese friends also asked Pat questions about Christianity. In a
short time, so many of Miriam's Buddhist friends had accepted Christ
that Pat started a Bible study for them. There sat Pat surrounded by
Chinese, Japanese, Filipino, and Vietnamese people with backgrounds
ranging from Buddhism to Greek Orthodoxy. An experienced Bible
study teacher, Pat began by using a detailed, verse-by-verse approach.
But it didn't work.

"They kept saying I went too fast, but I had slowed down," says
Pat. "When I prayed and asked God how I could reach them, the
phrase, *Go back,* kept coming to me." Pat thought it must mean to

teach more simple material. So she began teaching basic truths about Jesus from John's Gospel, but that wasn't simple enough either.

Still, as she prayed, the words *Go back* kept forming. She decided it meant to go back to third-grade-level teaching, which helped a bit. As she waited silently on God, she decided to make a time line beginning with Adam and Eve.

Pat told me this story while I was interviewing her for an article on Third World religions. After she finished, I explained how experts I'd interviewed the day before had told me that Buddhists and Hindus often regard Christianity as a "new" religion because it's only two thousand years old. "Help them understand that Christianity began with creation," I'd been told by the experts. "Look at the prophecies of Christ's coming, beginning with Adam and Eve." She and I marveled together at how she had done exactly the right thing based on what she'd heard in prayer.

When I asked if her prayer life was always so revealing, she said, "Only when I'm in deep, silent prayer, wanting only to do God's will. Only when I want nothing for myself, but only for Him." Selfless prayer that is focused on God—this is the heart of contemplation.

Stories like this may leave you wondering if contemplative prayer is even possible for you. In fact, contemplation is possible for anyone who is willing to try a few basic practices.

GETTING THERE

The truth is, you have already experienced fleeting moments of contemplation without calling it that. Have you sat staring at waves of the ocean? Or sat on a porch in the dark on a starry night, staring into space? Have you been stirred by a sermon, or in worship, so that you've felt as if you are staring into the shining face of God? Have you felt moved with awe during these times? Avery Brooke has written:

Deeper, wordless contemplation is something that we may experience either in church, in those blessed pauses between words, or in quiet times alone when we cease our words of prayer, put down our Bibles, and realize that God is both very near and familiar and yet beyond all knowing. We feel that we would like to know God so well that we could sit still for an hour in silent companionship, as with an old friend.[1]

Contemplation comes down to this: *paying attention to God.* Mary, sitting at the feet of Jesus, gives us a picture of contemplation because she was "wholly dedicated to the one thing necessary" (Luke 10:42). The author of *The Cloud of Unknowing* wrote that contemplation is "[striving] to fix your love on God forgetting all else. Center all your attention and desire on [the Lord] and *let this be* the sole concern of your mind and heart."[2]

Perhaps you've noticed the paradox that contemplation is both work and rest. You *strive* because it's hard work learning to be quiet before God. But with practice, it becomes rich and full. You *let it be* in the sense that you don't dare to engineer it, make it up, or invent a "spiritual experience." Then you risk deceiving yourself. Contemplative prayer is not about tingly experiences; rather, it centers in loving God and enjoying God's presence. The chief end of contemplation, wrote seventeenth-century Puritan theologian Richard Baxter, is "acquaintance and fellowship with God."[3]

Paying attention to God is similar to paying attention in a human love relationship. When you love someone, you think often about their good points: *He's so thoughtful. I've never met a more considerate person in my life.* In contemplation, we can also ponder God's magnanimous qualities—a love that never gives up on us, power to turn unjust situations around, the meekness to temper His power with mercy.

As we linger on a character quality—say, God's generosity—we long for that quality in ourselves. The more we admire Him, the more we desire to be generous and less greedy ourselves. And at the very next opportunity when we're called on to give sacrificially, we are more likely to give than to hold back because we have tasted and seen the goodness of God. This is why contemplation is neither oddly mystical nor boring. Rather, it's close to that familiar experience of "hanging out" or "just being with" someone, even if you are only doing mundane activities together. In our life with God, this is something of what it means to "practice the presence of God" as I live with Him as my companion even though I may never speak aloud to

Him that day. Not only is it possible, but it is satisfying to the soul to be with God in this way all day long (see 1 Thessalonians 5:17). It is possible to sense God's presence through the night (see Lamentations 2:19)—and to "arise in the morning," says Dallas Willard, "as hungry for God as for cornflakes and eggs."[4]

In this atmosphere of lingering with God and paying attention to Him, love for God grows. The key feature of contemplation is love. "It is love, or at least the desire to love, which must inspire the Christian to pray," wrote Jean-Nicholas Grou, an eighteenth-century priest who spent much of his adult life in exile because of political forces during the French Revolution. "It is the voice of the heart that prays. You ask what the voice of the heart is? It is love which is the voice of the heart. Love God and you will be always speaking to him."[5]

This results in great enjoyment of God. Once, I asked a friend to run an errand with me. I knew it would take forty-five minutes to drive each way, and I was feeling grouchy about wasting time that way. She came along with me and we talked nonstop for the first ten minutes. The rest of the way we were quiet. We weren't mad at each other, or even bored with each other. In fact, we thought we were having a good time. It's a wonderful experience to be quiet with someone and enjoy that person, just aware of her company, knowing you can draw upon her at any time. This is what wordless contemplation is often like. I *know* the God in whose presence I sit loves me. I *know* I am supremely valued. What could be better than that?

Conversations with God

As we taste and see God through this sort of prayer, we become eager for conversations with Him. We desire to spend time with God, having learned to like His company. When you're that hungry for God, a conversational life with Him becomes normal and natural.

In conversation, prayer moves beyond problem solving only, which is not just a trend of our psychology-oriented generation. In the past, Bernard of Clairvaux noted how we falsely love God "for His usefulness, not for Himself."[6] God has been reduced to a 911 emergency operator who quickly and cleverly cures all our ills. "Fixing what is broken or healing what is injured is indeed part of what the spiritual life is about," insists Wendy Wright. "But there is more. Spiritual seekers do not encounter human life as a problem to be solved but as a mystery to be entered and plumbed."[7]

This *God-is-more-than-problem-solver* view defies the notion some hold that Christians need problems to bring them closer to God. Supposedly, we pray more and feel closer to God in a crisis—so trouble's not so bad after all. It's as if spiritual growth is fueled only by 911 emergency calls to God, and so God is obliged to create frequent crises in our lives.

It's a radical thought to many Christians that they can have the same connection with God all the time that they sense during crisis moments. This has become my experience, but people ask me, "How does this happen?"

Our bond to God grows as we learn to continually "listen with the heart and mind opened wide," says Wright. "This invites us to be changed. To listen to [life's] depths is to find oneself on one's knees."[8] A listening heart and open mind allow constant contact with God. Dallas Willard affirms that "spiritual persons draw their life from a conversational relationship with God. They have 'a life beyond.'"[9] That *life beyond* invades all of earthly life—pulling us away from distractions, showing us how our character flaws are silly and useless, then drawing us into selfless service to Christ. The world becomes less centered in us and more centered in God.

The life beyond is charged with rich conversation with God, nourished by living in union with Him. Now, what Jesus said becomes clear:

> "Abide in me, and I in you. As the branch cannot bear fruit
> of itself, except it abide in the vine; no more can ye,
> except ye abide in me. I am the vine, ye are the branches:
> He that abideth in me, and I in him, the same bringeth
> forth much fruit: for without me ye can do nothing."
> (John 15:4-5, KJV)

Julian of Norwich, a fourteenth-century nun, said, in the old English of her day, "Our soul is made to be God's dwelling-place; and the dwelling-place of the soul is God. Prayer oneth the soul to God."[10]

"A Lively Longing for God"

Imagine for a moment that you are attending a seminar on prayer. What would the main points be? Often, prayer seminars are focused on learning "techniques" and "increasing effectiveness." The "bottom line"—getting prayers answered—is the big deal. In contemplative prayer, the emphasis shifts instead to these things:

Loving God. Contemplative prayer has no agenda except to "nourish in your heart the lively longing for God,"[11] the result of which is an "increasingly intimate fellowship with God."[12] Words are less important as we move into "the soul in paraphrase, the heart in pilgrimage," as poet George Herbert described prayer.[13]

Thomas Merton tells us, "We should not look for a 'method' or 'system,' but cultivate an 'attitude,' and 'outlook': faith, openness, attention, reverence, expectation, supplication, trust, joy."[14] If you cultivate those attitudes—faith, openness, attentiveness, and so on—God will work through your spirit and personality, and you'll invent your own how-tos for contemplative prayer.

Letting God set the agenda. Instead of approaching God with lists and requests, we simply "lay open our heart to God and beg Him to put into it whatever is most pleasing to him."[15]

When I first read the above statement by Jean-Nicholas Grou, I recalled being frustrated with my son earlier that morning. So I tried to do as Grou suggested and I prayed Grou's words: *Put into my heart whatever is most pleasing to You.* As I opened my heart for God's reshaping, I could let God replace my frustration with grace and tenderness. The task that seemed so impossible earlier that morning (letting go of the frustration) now seemed simple. Open-hearted paying attention to God allows God to set the agenda and address the things in our heart that need change and direction.

Is God Really *Here*?

Contemplative prayer won't make much sense unless you believe in the depths of your soul and the practical, cynical parts of your personality that God is actually present. On certain levels, we're not sure God is here. We can't see Him, can't touch Him. Worship leaders sometimes talk about "coming into God's presence" as if we'd left it. It's as though a logician exists in the back of our mind who says,"It's okay to pray to someone no one can see, but to *listen* for a response and to expect companionship from this invisible someone is insanity." This is why we need to cultivate an awareness that God is truly present with us.

Scripture assures us that God is present everywhere at the same time: "If I go up to the heavens, you are there; if I make my bed in the depths, you are there. If I rise on the wings of the dawn, if I settle on the far side of the sea, even there your hand will guide me" (Psalm 139:8-10).

God's constant presence shows how He created us to be with Him and for His delight. Can you see God's delight in these scenes?

- God talked with Moses, a flawed but diligent seeker: "The LORD would speak to Moses face to face, as a man speaks with his friend" (Exodus 33:11).
- "Enoch walked with God" (Genesis 5:24). I wonder—did they converse, or walk together in silence? Or did Enoch do all the talking, as we do?
- After Paul, the mass murderer, was converted and received his call from God to preach to the Gentiles, he went to Arabia for three years instead of "consult[ing] any man." What did God think of this man who turned his heart so decidedly for Him? (See Galatians 1:16-18.)
- David sang about how, after running for years from Saul, God "brought me out into a spacious place; he rescued me because he delighted in me" (Psalm 18:19).
- Ruth cared for her mother-in-law and gleaned in fields under God's open skies to feed them both. Boaz sensed God's pleasure: "May you be richly rewarded by the LORD, the God of Israel, under whose wings you have come to take refuge" (Ruth 2:12).

Only because we are unable to see God with our fallen eyes do we invent the idea of "visiting" God now and then at church, retreats, and official moments of prayer. When we talk about "entering God's presence," we speak as if there are places where God is not. I think of this as the "Jonah myth." Jonah seemed to believe that God would not be present on a ship headed for Nineveh, yet he learned that God was there . . . and even present in the digestive tract of a great animal. I've made my own list of places where I seem to believe that God is not: answering the seventh telemarketer phone call during a Sunday nap, standing in front of a full-length mirror in a fitting room trying on swimming attire, being asked to hold a plate of doughnuts when you're on a diet. At those moments, God seems absent. So we can sympathize with Jonah. What do we make of God's invisibility to us on earth?

It's true that God is above and apart from us, and that He is distinctly different from us. We speak of His transcendence, meaning that God is above the world and separated from it by an impassable gulf. But God is also absolutely near, and in Christ He has become like us so that we might become like Him. We speak of His immanence, meaning that God is present in all His works, including the world. If you raise your hand now in the air, God is in that space. Tozer writes:

> There is no place where [God] is not. . . . Ten million intelligences standing at as many points in space and separated by incomprehensible distances can each say with equal truth, God is here. Always, everywhere, God is present, and always He seeks to discover Himself to each one of us.[16]

The problem is not that God goes away, but that we are unaware of His presence. Yet Paul said to us all, including unbelievers: "God is not far from each one of us. 'For in him we live and move and have our being'" (Acts 17:27-28). Be assured that a sharper awareness comes through faith. You don't have to make up a sense of God's presence or pretend that He's really there. "To [the convinced Christian]," writes Tozer, "'the practice of the presence of God' consists not of projecting an imaginary object from within his own mind and then seeking to realize its presence; rather it is to recognize the real presence of the One whom all sound theology declares to be already there. The resultant experience is not visionary but real."[17]

THE GOD WHO SHOWS UP

The more contemplation teaches you to pay attention to God, the easier it becomes to be aware of His presence. In fact, God begins showing up in places that don't resemble a church sanctuary or a wooded glen. If you set your heart to pay attention to God, who is indeed present, depend upon this: *God will invade even the unlikely moments of life.*

Quite unintentionally, I began a spiritual discipline of worship, confession, and contemplative prayer when I started walking aerobically down a canyon road. It got rather boring, however, so I began listening to a worship tape and enjoyed it so much I found that certain songs called for a twirl now and then. But the real me also began showing up on these walks, and I obsessed on who did what to me and how I would love to tell off a few people. Suddenly, I'd catch myself in the middle of a bitter diatribe. Then I'd feel shame at forgetting God and focusing on whomever I was annoyed with—until I began to see things in a different light. What if God was stirring up my soul when I was with Him, so the ugliness I harbored within could come to the surface in the light of His presence? What if He wanted to lead me through confession? Now I see that God brings my "enemies" to this canyon road sanctuary and together we pay attention to them, practicing what it means to love the people I would otherwise loathe.

The best thing about these canyon road walks is that God waits on me, inviting my attention back when it wanders. On that walk and in my life, God sits at a table that is always ready and waiting for me. I am a guest, being welcomed by God as in that picturesque phrase of Psalm 23: "You prepare a table before me in the presence of my enemies. You anoint my head with oil; my cup overflows" (verse 5). When I start yammering about my frustrations, God doesn't get up and leave. God invites me to return to Him in conversation and anoints me again.

If we choose to *be present* to God—and give God permission to speak—we can expect God to show up. It surprised me to meet God while wearing sweat clothes and a hot pink baseball cap, but perhaps God saw that canyon road as a place where He could get my attention.

I work very hard in my head all day, and when I exercise, my mind relaxes. There, where I was vulnerable to the heat, dodging the gravel trucks, and devoid of complex thoughts, God could find in me a ready ear to hear.

What is it that will make you more ready to live and walk in the presence of God?

How Far Will You Go with God?

As we close this chapter, I ask you to be open to the ways—perhaps some of them new—God calls you to pray. Allow Him a wider range of possibilities in what He wants to say to you. Don't limit your life with God to what you've read elsewhere or will read in this book. Depend on our God who is always present to keep showing up and making His presence known to you.

Before moving on to the next chapter, it will help you to pause now and consider these questions:

- How open to God are you? How open would you like to be?
- You may believe God listens, but do you believe God speaks?
- What are the greatest distractions that keep you from believing God is always present?
- What would make prayer more attractive to you?

Notes
1. Avery Brooke, "What Is Contemplation?" *Weavings*, July/August 1992, p. 9.
2. Fr. James Walsh, ed., *The Cloud of Unknowing* (Rahwey, NJ: Paulist Press, 1981), p. 49.
3. Richard Baxter, *The Saints' Everlasting Rest*, as quoted in "editor's introduction," John Mogabgab *Weavings,* July/August 1992, p. 2.
4. Dallas Willard, *In Search of Guidance: Developing a Conversational Relationship with God* (San Francisco: HarperSanFrancisco, 1993), p. 234.
5. Jean-Nicholas Grou, *How to Pray* (Cambridge, England: James Clarke & Co., 1955), pp. 38, 18, 19.
6. Bernard of Clairvaux, *Great Devotional Classics: Revelations of Divine Love*, ed. Douglas V. Steere (Nashville, TN: The Upper Room, 1961), p. 15.
7. Wendy Wright, "Desert Listening," *Weavings,* May/June 1994, pp. 13-14.
8. Wright, p. 14.

9. Willard, p. 239.
10. Julian of Norwich, *Great Devotional Classics: Revelations of Divine Love*, ed. Constance Garrett (Nashville, TN: The Upper Room, 1963), pp. 26, 30.
11. *The Cloud of Unknowing*, p. 47.
12. Baxter, as quoted in Mogabgab, *Weavings*, p. 2.
13. George Herbert, "Prayer," *Great Sonnets*, ed. Paul Negri (New York: Dover Publications, 1994), p. 20.
14. Thomas Merton, *Contemplative Prayer* (New York: Doubleday, Image Books, 1996), p. 34.
15. Grou, p. 18.
16. A. W. Tozer, *The Pursuit of God* (Camp Hill, PA: Christian Publications, Inc., 1982), pp. 62, 64.
17. A. W. Tozer, *The Knowledge of the Holy* (San Francisco: HarperSanFrancisco, 1961), p. 76.

CHAPTER
6

A HEART THAT LISTENS

G OD IS THE ONE WHO KEEPS SHOWING UP AND IS ALWAYS PRESENT to us, but we need to recognize that He's at the door trying to get our attention.

How can we be more alert to Him? The fact is, we do not need to be monks or mystics in order to cultivate a lifestyle that makes us more perceptive of God.

THE CONTEMPLATIVE WAY

The two primary tools of the contemplative way are the spiritual disciplines of *silence* and *solitude*.

These are not the pastimes people enjoy most. In fact, both are undervalued in our culture. Quiet people are urged to assert themselves. Those who do speak up are urged to do so more eloquently. Can you imagine an adult education catalog featuring a class titled "Learning to Be Quiet"? Usually we are plugged into headphones, tuned in to the radio, transfixed by a book, or mesmerized by a TV show. Even at church, where we've been taught to pray, does anyone teach us how to be quiet in the presence of God?

Our culture mistakenly believes that *silence* means you are *weak* or that you have nothing to say. But Madame Jeanne Guyon, a sought-after counselor and author of the seventeenth-century classic *Experiencing the Depths of Jesus Christ*, wrote that two kinds of people keep silent:

> The first is one who has nothing to say, and the other is one who has too much to say. In the case of the deeper encounter with the Lord, the latter is true. Silence is produced from [abundant life in God], not from lack. This silence is rich, full, and alive![1]

Solitude is also not popular. It appears to be lonely isolation. But solitude is not being alone—it is being alone *with God*. This is vastly different from isolation because we have for companionship the One who loves us and who is eager to empower us to do His will. Avery Brooke writes, "We feel that we would like to know God so well that we could sit still for an hour in silent companionship, as with an old friend."[2]

In fact, learning the spiritual discipline of solitude is the antidote to loneliness, says author Elisabeth Elliot. She became well-acquainted with loneliness after the death of her first husband, martyred missionary Jim Elliot. She offers this advice from her experience: "Turn your loneliness into solitude, and your solitude into prayer."[3] With God as companion, loneliness becomes a sweet solitude in which we can pour out our heart to God. "Loneliness is a wilderness," she observes, "but through accepting it from the hand of God, and offering it back to Him with thanksgiving, it may become a pathway to God Himself."[4]

THE WORK OF SILENCE AND SOLITUDE

Silence and solitude both work in hidden ways, resembling the work that goes on during winter. In the cold months, it appears nothing is going on. Animals hibernate. Nothing grows. Everything is still and at rest. But in the important sleep of winter, life renews itself. In silence and solitude, God works in ways that are hidden, but nevertheless vital to life.

Part of the vital work that is done in silence and solitude is *detach-*

ing ourselves from the demands of our culture. In the absence of urgent messages and ringing telephones, we see self-promotion for what it is. We create a space in which the spiritual characteristics of Christ can grow within us. And out of this growing, transforming spirit, we begin *responding* to life rather than *reacting* to it. From our quiet time apart we *gain* inner silence, and that frees us from the world. It equips us to grow as the person God is forming us to be. Solitude is not a means of escape for people who can't handle life: "Solitude is not turning one's back on the world; it is turning our face toward God."[5]

Both silence and solitude require discipline at first, but then they become enjoyable and refreshing. After attending his first silent retreat, one man reported, "What a relief. I never knew how draining it was to make small-talk, how it shifted my focus from God to myself as I wondered what other people were thinking about me." Silence and solitude disentangle us from what society calls success: cheering crowds, financial gain, glitzy comebacks, and perpetually happy faces. Once again, God uses things considered "foolish" (unlikely) "to confound the wise" (1 Corinthians 1:27, KJV).

TOO DIFFICULT?

But if silence and solitude are so foreign to our culture, won't contemplative prayer be too difficult? Only if you choose to make it so. "Seek nothing from God during these quiet moments except to love Him and please Him,"[6] writes Madame Guyon. And it gets more simple, not more complex, as we go along, Thomas Kelly assures us.[7] It is not an arduous task, but "nothing more than turning our heart toward God and receiving in turn His love."[8]

Contemplation is so simple that it can work for the average person with a headache. One morning in Sunday school I had a cold, and the rousing discussion made my head ache more. I considered going home to lie down but decided to first sit quietly and enjoy the presence of God. I slipped into the sanctuary and sat in a pew under the balcony where it was dark and no one could see me. I shut my eyes and listened to the worship team practice. The piano keys rolled out their flowing tune. The bass player thumped out his part, and the recorder squeaked repeatedly over difficult parts, creating a cacophony of sounds that would have made me wince if I hadn't been absolutely present to God. Because my head hurt, I couldn't pray in words, but I could sit there and love God, enjoying how His children worshiped even when they were only practicing. It's as if I were "plunged into a river of peace."[9]

Certainly there are days when I'm so agitated I find contemplation difficult. It is then that I'm humbled and pleased to know I am not the only seeker. For God is in the business of seeking us out. When Israel strayed from Him, God said, "I will give them a heart to know me" (Jeremiah 24:7). *God, give me a heart to know You!*

Turning Our Face Toward God

In solitary silence, we encounter the love of God. "In this silence, God pours into you a deep, inward love," wrote Madame Guyon, who speaks from her experience of enjoying God's presence in the more than twenty years she spent in prison and exile for her beliefs in having a personal relationship with God.[10] "This experience of love is one that will fill and permeate your whole being. [It] is the beginning of an indescribable blessedness."[11]

God makes His presence rich and full by being a good host and doing the master-of-ceremonies work. After we've acquired a knack for quietness, God is the initiator, "stirring within people a response to Him. There is no path to God that is not first God's path to us."[12] We love because He first loved us (see 1 John 4:19). The question is not "How am I to find God?" but "How am I to let myself be found by Him?"[13]

Why does God use silence to touch us? Because God is not domineering and does not ordinarily force people to pay attention to Him. We become so busy running our lives that we become oblivious of the Spirit of God: "It requires a lot of inner solitude and silence to become aware of these divine movements. God does not shout, scream or push"[14] (although we accuse Him of doing so).

The Surrendered Heart

Yet solitary silence is not all sweetness and light: it can be jarring and disturbing.

Even this is good because it forces us to shift from our normal course of conscious thinking in our wordy, noisy world. We're forced to stop measuring ourselves by others and by the world's standards, and to consider the "life beyond." Silence and solitude are outward, physical manifestations of the inward surrender of the heart. We relinquish talking, analyzing, and enjoying the company of others in order to attend only to God.

This relinquishment is crucial. "We have all heard this holy Whisper at times," wrote Thomas Kelly, a Quaker college professor and spiritual leader of post-World War I relief workers in Germany. "Only at times have we submitted to His holy guidance. We have not counted this Holy Thing within us to be the most precious thing in the world. We have not surrendered *all else*, to attend to it alone."[15]

That "all else" to be surrendered includes not only talking and the company of others but also the desire to manage and control our prayer time. Contemplative prayer involves no lists of requests, no outline for structure, no opening and closing. This is a true conversation—I am not in charge.

Trying hard to be good at contemplative prayer may even sabotage it. "When you come to the Lord, learn to have a quiet mind. Cease from any self-effort. In this way, God Himself can act all alone,"[16] wrote Madame Guyon. Wise souls will find it a relief to no longer be "pleasantly attached to their own efforts."[17]

Contemplative prayer requires that we put away that "looking good, kid" image within us that tries so hard to be good, and instead be our true self before God—vulnerable and naked. We take the yet-to-be-transformed parts of ourselves (self-sufficient attitudes, materialistic desires) and surrender them to God instead of stashing them in a closet. The surrendered will and attentive mind says, "You know my faults. You love me. I give this person, troublesome situation, or grievous sin to you." David, the psalmist, said of himself, "My sin is ever before me" not because he was beating himself up or had low self-esteem, but because he had sat under the examinations of God and acquired a realistic assessment of his flawed humanness.

Vulnerability to God strips us of our need to protect our "looking good, kid" image because we feel surrounded and protected by Him, as He becomes our soul's "refuge" and "mighty fortress" (see Psalm 46). In this safe place, we can lay aside our natural need to protect ourselves from the attacks of others. We also become aware of the fact that we care for people largely because they give us special attention, single us out for praise, or do favors for us.

And so solitary, silent experiences call for a rigorous emptying of self. I can't dazzle God with words, I just *am* before God. Thomas Merton wrote the following about virtue, which I have paraphrased to apply to prayer: "A [person] who is not stripped and poor and naked within his own soul will unconsciously tend to *pray prayers* for his own sake rather than for the glory of God. He will be *prayerful* not because he loves God's will but because he wants to admire his own *prayerfulness*."[18]

This piercing vulnerability pushes us to die to our self-love and become "broken bread and poured-out wine in the hands of Jesus Christ."[19] Madame Guyon wrote, "Prayer is a melting. Prayer is a dissolving and an uplifting of the soul."[20] As our willfulness melts our misshapen self-obsession, there's a blending of self with God.

In that "melting," we no longer *need* to be clever and wonderful in order to prove our acceptability. I wrote to my friend who was coordinating a silent retreat and expressed my fears about my ability to lead it well. She wrote back: "The wonderful thing about silent retreats is God's ability to work by His Holy Spirit without us being His Holy Spirit. You will be fine." She was right. I didn't have to make others' spiritual experiences happen, the Holy Spirit would. I would only set the tone so that people were likely to be attentive to God's presence in their lives. All that clamoring for attention and recognition—mine and theirs—could be put to rest. "But I have stilled and quieted my soul; like a weaned child with its mother, like a weaned child is my soul within me" (Psalm 131:2).

This contentment is frequent in silent, solitary prayer. We stop using prayer to control people and circumstances. Satisfaction comes as we let go of inadequacies ("Oh no, I'm not praying. I'm drifting, I'm distracted"). Instead of focusing on our errors in prayer, we see that prayer is about God, not us.

Surrender eventually permeates the way you make prayer requests. You can't rattle them off without seeing yourself banging on the vending-machine image of God. Your first priority is no longer to get what you want, but to listen to the heart of God and see what God wants. You still make requests—which are part of our relationship with God and honored by God—but surrendering to God is now the bigger issue.

WHAT THE LISTENING HEART HEARS

A surrendered heart, trained by silence and solitude, listens, which means it sees and hears what others don't. When Aram's soldiers, horses, and chariots came after Elisha, they surrounded the city. Elisha and his servant got up the next morning and saw the armies, but only the servant was afraid. Why? "Those who are with us are more than those who are with them." And Elisha prayed, "O LORD, open his eyes so he may see." Then the Lord opened the servant's eyes, and he saw the hills full of horses and chariots of fire all around Elisha (see 2 Kings 6:16-17). When I get into confusing situations, I often imagine those chariots of fire and ask God for a heart that sees what God is up to and the ability to respond to it.

Having a listening heart isn't just for the spiritual elite. It's for all. Joan of Arc (in George Bernard Shaw's play "Saint Joan") made this clear to Charles, king of France, when he was annoyed that God spoke to this peasant girl but not to him. "Oh, your voices, your voices," he sniped at her. "Why don't the voices come to me? I am king, not you."

Joan answered, "The [voices] do come to you; but you do not hear them. When the angelus rings you cross yourself and have done with it; but *if you prayed from your heart*, and listened to the thrilling of the bells in the air after they stop ringing, you would hear the voices as well as I do."[21] As the angelus bells rang several times a day calling the townspeople to prayer standing wherever they were, Joan stopped to listen to God with her heart, but the king paid his respects and moved on. Listening from the heart puts us in a hushed place in which waves of love and adoration wash over us: "Our spirit is on tiptoe—alert and listening."[22]

And it's a different sort of listening—"not listening to words, to arguments, to pros and cons, to positions and opinions. It involves listening to the delicate intersection of the human heart, with its desires and dreams, and the vast and silent mystery that is God."[23] This God-human juncture can occur in all kinds of quiet. It may be solitary contemplation or the cultivated inner quiet that goes with us even to a hockey game or board meeting, as we momentarily pull away from the chaos and listen to the heart of God.

Entering In

As silence and solitude become more important in the way you communicate with God, you start making space in your life because you want to. You long to be with God in a more focused way.

After enjoying seven months in a quiet abbey, Henri Nouwen pondered how he would survive in the hectic world of university teaching and guest lecturing. He saw that he needed to make concrete decisions about silence, solitude, and prayer. So he set up a routine of regular times of reflection and retreat days, but he was advised that these would not be enough. He would also need prayer as a daily discipline, especially the integration of prayer with his work.

What changes have to occur in your lifestyle to make solitude a priority in your life? If you're active in this world, you need a plan to build Sabbath contemplation into your life. Nouwen advised not to move too fast: "It is better to have a daily practice of ten minutes [of] solitude than to have a whole hour once in awhile."[24]

Retreat days are universally recommended. As you set aside time to reflect quietly, ask God to show you what you need to do during these "sabbatical" days. These used to scare me. I wondered, "What will I do?" So I began pitching ideas into a file folder I kept on my desk—questions to ask God, goals to ponder, decisions to make, books and articles to read. Then I *listened to God* until that appointed day came nearer, asking, "What are you calling me to do on my sabbatical days?" This sort of preparation helps us become ready and excited about connecting with God in a more intense way during times of extended solitude. You may take along the tools you'll need (Bible, prayer books, journals) but don't obsess on them. I take the file folder with me, but often I never open it. I let the day work itself out.

For a retreat, it helps to go to a retreat center, monastery, or campground. For one-day outings, one friend goes to a little-used park and simply sits there. Another stays at home when everyone else is gone. Multiple days—even a few weeks—are better. If you can't possibly do any of this, try an hour in the backyard of your home or balcony of your apartment and do it as soon as you can. See what happens. Keep seeking ways to internalize Scripture so it will form Christ's character in you. This may include meditating on a passage that speaks to your soul's neediness so that you more eagerly depend on God, or it may involve a repeated reading of the Gospels so that you absorb the boldness and charity of Jesus.

Be aware that your retreat day will probably not go well if you have not had days off recently. We all need days of "serious nothing," in which no activities are scheduled and we can do whatever comes to mind—sleeping, going to the beach, cleaning out the garage. If you come to your retreat day physically spent, those needs will take over and sabotage the purpose of your retreat day. We don't retreat well when we're not rested.

After you've tried a few retreat days, expect your hunger for God in silence and solitude to increase. With that longing for God and taste of detachment, it will be easier to let go of activities and pare down commitments. You will become more intentional in what you do because you will be driven not by the culture, but by the heart of God. The disciplines that once seemed so distasteful—being alone with God, being quiet—may even become favorite pastimes.

WALKING WITH GOD FOR LIFE

Eventually, silence and solitude, the chief communication skills in the way we interact with God, become a delight, not a burden. As we finish this chapter, consider the words of author Phillip Keller:

> For the man or woman who has come to know and love the Lord God in the depths of such intimacy, the times of solitude are the most precious in all of life. They are a rendezvous with the Beloved. They are anticipated with eagerness—gentle interludes with [God] alone are highlights of life.[25]

Notes

1. Jeanne Guyon, *Experiencing the Depths of Jesus Christ* (Beaumont, TX: The SeedSowers, 1975), p. 61.

2. Avery Brooke, "What Is Contemplation?" *Weavings*, July/August 1992, p. 9.

3. Elisabeth Elliot, "Turning Solitude into Prayer," *Cross Point,* Summer 1997, p. 7.

4. Elliot, p. 7.

5. Thomas Merton, *New Seeds of Contemplation* (New York: New Directions, 1962), pp. 52-63, and Henri Nouwen, *Reaching Out: The Movements of the Spiritual Life* (New York: Doubleday, 1975), pp. 37-62 as developed and adapted by David Rensberger in "The Holiness of Winter," *Weavings*, November/December 1996, p. 40.

6. Madame Guyon, *Experiencing God through Prayer,* ed. Donna Arthur (Springdale, PA: Whitaker House, 1984), p. 24.

7. Thomas Kelly, *A Testament of Devotion* (New York: Walker and Company, 1987), p. 59.

8. Guyon, p. 11.

9. Jan Johnson, *Madame Guyon* (Minneapolis, MN: Bethany House Publishers, 1999), p. 81.

10. Jan Johnson, *Madame Guyon*

11. Jeanne Guyon, *Experiencing the Depths of Jesus Christ*, p. 60.

12. *Great Devotional Classics: Bernard of Clairvaux*, ed. Douglas Steere (Nashville, TN: The Upper Room, 1961), p. 5.

13. Henri Nouwen, *The Return of the Prodigal Son* (New York: Doubleday, 1992), p. 106.

14. Henri Nouwen, "Deeper Into Love," *Weavings*, September/October 1995, p. 25.

15. Kelly, p. 159

16. Jeanne Guyon, *Experiencing the Depths of Jesus Christ,* p. 60.

17. Jeanne Guyon, *Experiencing the Depths of Jesus Christ,* p. 60.

18. Thomas Merton, *New Seeds of Contemplation* (New York: New Directions, 1962), p. 58. Merton wrote, "A [person] who is not stripped and poor and naked within his own soul will unconsciously tend to *do* the *works* he has to do for his own sake rather than for the glory of God. He will be *virtuous* not because he loves God's will but because he wants to admire his own *virtues.*" I have substituted a form of the word "prayer" for the italicized words above.

19. Oswald Chambers, *My Utmost for His Highest* (Westwood, NJ: Barbour and Company, Inc., 1963), p. 40.

20. Jeanne Guyon, *Experiencing the Depths of Jesus Christ,* p. 88.

21. Warren S. Smith, ed., *Bernard Shaw's Plays* (New York: W.W. Norton & Company, Inc., 1970), Scene V, p. 190.

22. Richard Foster, *Prayer: Finding the Heart's True Home* (San Francisco: HarperSanFrancisco, 1992), p. 163.

23. Wendy Wright, "Desert Listening," *Weavings,* May/June 1994, p. 11.

24. Henri Nouwen, *Making All Things New* (San Francisco: Harper San Francisco, 1981), p. 79.

25. W. Phillip Keller, "Solitude for Serenity and Strength," *Decision Magazine,* August/September 1981, p. 8, as quoted in Joyce Huggett, *The Joy of Listening to God* (Downers Grove, IL: InterVarsity Press, 1986), p. 64.

THE ALERT SOUL

Perhaps you wonder if you could be still before God without dozing off or losing interest. Is it possible to be peaceful, yet alert? This is a legitimate concern.

The first time I taught on meditation and contemplative prayer, I had serious concerns. Would the men and women in the workshop be able to sit still long enough to contemplate? Would they fall asleep? After all, we are productive people who don't pause for long, so when we do, we tend to doze off.

After I explained the process to the retreat participants, they moved into the positions I suggested and shut their eyes. It got quiet. There was some shifting, clearing of throats, and finally only the hum of the lights. I prayed the dullness of their wait would grow into an awareness of God. Their subsequent reports of experiencing God astounded me.

One of the things that struck me during this process was the look on their faces as they began. Their closed eyes and relaxed mouths displayed peace, yet their uplifted chins and even raised eyebrows revealed expectancy and alertness. You'd think that peace and alertness couldn't be found in the same person, but I saw this profound mixture in their faces and body language.

In the beginning, it takes some time to learn how to "center" yourself. By this I mean bringing your thoughts and attention to the center of your being—into your heart, where you can listen to what's going on in your soul. To do this requires us to detach from the world's concerns, including all those inner voices in our head that tell us we should be washing down the driveway or cooking dinner. This detachment, however, is not rigid. As Richard Foster says, "This is not suppressing our inner turmoil but letting go of it. Suppression implies a pressing down, a keeping in check, whereas in recollection we are giving away, releasing."[1] Little by little, as we let go of concerns surrounding us, we *focus on God's presence* and attach ourselves there. We're not forcing anything but placing ourselves in a setting in which we're likely to hear God.

What does it mean to focus on God's presence?

At first, it means to agree intellectually that God is present and that His presence is a good thing. With more practice, that initial intellectual assent grows into an awareness of the all-powerful God who loves us. In time, we develop a *sense* of the divine presence. I can think of no better word than *sense* because it is beyond thinking or feeling. Sometimes it encompasses both, but it is bigger than merely thinking or feeling. Other times, it involves neither because it's simply a way of *being,* this sense that you are surrounded by, or centered in, God Himself.

Perhaps the best way to describe centering oneself in God is that we move over to God's wavelength, agreeing to think the kinds of thoughts He thinks. Centering has two purposes: It calms and quiets us so we can better enjoy God's presence, and it makes us alert to God.

This experience, sometimes called "abiding" in God, was described well by missionary Amy Carmichael, whose spiritual vision kept her strong in the face of people's threats and abandonment by her own mission board:

Keep close, keep close. If you are close you will be keen.
Your heart will be set on the things that abide. You will
drink of His Spirit and you will thirst for souls even as He
thirsts. You will not be attracted by the world that crucified

Him, but you will love the people in that world who have never seen His beauty and are losing so much more than they know. You will live to share your joy in Him. Nothing else will count for much.[2]

Nothing else in this world.

HELP IN CENTERING

When we first attempt contemplation, it helps our restless minds get settled if we do it in the same place each time. It might be a quiet corner of a room or a park bench facing a garden or a chair facing a window of plants in an apartment. Once you get accustomed to contemplative prayer, you can practice it to some degree anywhere you are — in your car as you wait for a friend or during an airplane flight.

Body position can also make a difference in the ability to center oneself, especially in the beginning. The classic position is to sit in a straight-back chair with feet flat on the floor and with the palms of the hands turned up in a gesture of receptivity and surrender. This is wise because crossing arms or legs means you'll be interrupted in a few minutes with a cramp or a limb going to sleep. Choose a position in which you can be still because moving is such a distraction. I like sitting on the floor with my back straight against the wall. I've observed others lie on the floor on their back — or on their face, which was Jesus' position in Gethsemane (see Matthew 26:39; 2 Chronicles 20:18; Daniel 6:10, 8:18). Whatever position you choose, keep in mind that your purpose is to put into practice the truth that your very being is a dwelling place for the Almighty.

As you begin to pray, your body may require an overt action to help in centering. This may be the use of one of the "breath" prayers. One of these is "More of Jesus (breathe in), less of me (breathe out)." Another centering technique is the "palms up, palms down method," described by Richard Foster:

> Begin by placing your palms down as a symbolic indication of your desire to turn over any concerns you may have to God. Inwardly you may pray, "Lord, I give to You my anger toward John. I release my fear of my dentist

appointment this morning. I surrender my anxiety over not having enough money to pay the bills this month. I release my frustration over trying to find a baby-sitter for tonight." Whatever it is that weighs on your mind or is a concern to you, just say, "Palms down." Release it. After several moments of surrender, turn your palms up as a symbol of your desire to receive from the Lord. Perhaps you will pray silently: "Lord, I would like to receive Your divine love for John, Your peace about the dentist appointment, Your patience, Your joy."[3]

Scripture phrases or scenes can help us center ourselves. Madame Guyon called this "beholding the Lord": "It is not that you will think about what you have read, but you will *feed* upon what you have read. Out of a love for the Lord you exert your will to hold your mind quiet before Him. In this peaceful state, *swallow* what you have tasted, and take in what is there as nourishment."[4] That nourishment makes the soul come back for more.

A. W. Tozer used the image of the Holy of Holies for centering:

Where above the mercy seat dwelt the very God Himself in awful and glorious manifestation. While the tabernacle stood, only the high priest could enter there, and that but once a year, with blood which he offered for his sins and the sins of the people. It was this last veil which was rent when our Lord gave up the ghost on Calvary, and the sacred writer explains that this rending of the veil opened the way for every worshipper in the world to come by the new and living way straight into the divine Presence.

Tozer went on to say, "God wills that we should push on into His presence and live our whole life there."[5]

A Key Word or Phrase

To ease into the quiet, it may help to repeat a certain word. This repetition is not a chant to empty the mind of logic and reason. Quite the opposite; it is a way to fill the mind with God, and God alone. It may help to use the same word each time, such as: God, Jesus, peace. For those who are concerned about the Bible's warning against "vain repetition" in prayer (see Matthew 6:7), consider that the repetition need not be meaningless, but it can help us focus better and dig deeper. The repetition can in fact be soothing and very freeing, helping us, as Nouwen says, "to empty out our crowded interior life and create the quiet space where we can dwell with God."[6]

Begin with simple, whispered words, advises Thomas Kelly:

> Formulate them spontaneously, "Thine only. Thine only."
> Or seize upon a fragment of the Psalms: "So panteth my
> soul after Thee, O God." Repeat them inwardly, over and
> over again. If you wander, return and begin again. But the
> time will come when verbalization is not so imperative,
> and yields place to the attitudes of soul which you meant
> the words to express, attitudes of humble bowing before
> Him, attitudes of lifting high your whole being before Him
> that the Light may shine into the last crevice and drive
> away all darkness. If you find, after a time, that these atti-
> tudes become diffused and vague, no longer firm-textured,
> then return to verbalizations and thus restore their solidity.[7]

Words can help us begin; words can help us come back when we wander.

You may wish to use a familiar scriptural phrase, such as "for me to live is Christ" or "to know Christ" or "Christ lives in me" (Philippians 1:21, 3:10; Galatians 2:20). In the beginning, I centered myself with "Lord, fill my mind with Your peace, and my heart with Your love" because it seemed my mind was never peaceful and my heart was never loving. Now, that prayer is too wordy for me when I'm centering.

Perhaps the most frequently used phrase is the ancient "Jesus prayer": "Lord Jesus Christ, have mercy on me, a sinner." This combines words from two scriptural incidents (see Luke 18:13, Matthew 20:30-31).

I sometimes offer the phrase "I am here," as a paraphrase of "Here I am." Abraham, Jacob, Moses, Samuel, and Isaiah said these words.

These were even Jesus' words to the Father (see Hebrews 2:13, 10:7, 10:9) and to the churches (see Revelation 3:20). To go before God and declare "Here I am! It's me, again" is a treat reserved for those with a listening heart.

SINGING

Singing helps our bodies do what is needed in centering: to breathe in and out deeply and to relax the parts of ourselves we don't realize are tense. At a retreat where I was speaking, the retreat committee members seemed difficult to deal with. I prayed for them but their disharmony wore me out. I was unable to be at peace. After I sent the attendees to discussion groups, I sat down to pray as I usually do during this time. I couldn't get beyond muttering to God about this committee.

I saw the piano and remembered how I used to relax myself as a teenager by playing the piano. So I opened the hymnal and played several hymns I hadn't heard since those teen years of playing in church. I began searching for "Dear Lord and Father of Mankind" because I wanted to sing that line "Forgive our foolish ways." I found it and played it seven or eight times. With my mind and body thus quieted, I put my hands in my lap and sat on the bench in silence. When the retreat participants returned, my heart was reconciled to all of them—even the committee. I was able to interact with the group in peace.

Singing songs of praise works especially well. William Law was a seventeenth-century Englishman denied the priesthood in the Anglican church because he would not swear allegiance to a monarch who ascended the throne unfairly. In his classic book, *A Serious Call to a Holy and Devout Life*, he writes:

> There is nothing that so clears a way for your prayers,
> nothing that so disperses dullness of heart, nothing that so
> purifies the soul from poor and little passions, nothing that
> so opens heaven or carries your heart so near it as these
> songs of praise. They create a sense of delight in God;
> they awaken holy desires; they teach how to ask; and they
> prevail with God to give. They kindle a holy flame; they

turn your heart into an altar; they turn your prayers into incense and carry them as sweet smelling savor to the throne of grace.[8]

It seems William Law fully expected the heavens to open to him in prayer, dispersing dryness and releasing him from petty thoughts. His words assure us this is possible.

Be aware that God may reveal to you your own method of centering. It would not be unlike God to see your uniqueness and lead you into abiding in Him in your own way. Here is a method Madeleine L'Engle uses:

> I have memorized an alphabet of prayers and hymns, which I sing or say to myself very slowly. And they're all words that mean something to me. And if I just stay with those words very quietly, they help put me out of the way and get me in the right state of mind.[9]

HANDLING DISTRACTIONS

Depend on it: As you center yourself in God, you will finally remember all those dratted things you forgot in the previous twenty-four hours—calling the pharmacy or taking your vitamins! Like distracted Martha, we have preparations to make, and there's nothing like quieting yourself to bring them up.

Occasionally, we're even distracted by a temptation—something so out of place and bizarre it's jarring. Other times, it's so cunning you don't even realize it. It might concern food or sex or the plumbing or your wardrobe. It's tempting to beat ourselves up, but it works better to turn our attention immediately back to God.

Madame Guyon gave wise advice about distractions: "Do not become distressed because your mind has wandered away. Always guard yourself from being anxious because of your faults. Such distress only stirs up the soul and distracts you to outward things. Your distress really springs from a secret root of pride."[10] The pride comes from thinking we're above being distracted.

Madame Guyon's advice not to fight distractions directly works because you can't *fight* distractions away. If you try, you waste your energy. Distress over distractions becomes even more distracting! It's a losing battle. It's better to keep paper and pen nearby and capture distractions on paper (much like a "to-do" list) and let them go. (Often when I'm finished praying, the day is outlined—and sometimes great ideas have occurred as I've done this.) Madame Guyon's antidote was positive: "Turn within, again and again, no matter how often you are drawn away."[11] So we don't think, *My mind shouldn't be wandering*, but, *God is present*. The more you center yourself, the easier it becomes.

Now and then, an interfering thought is a topic for contemplation. So I begin with "What do I need to know about this doctor's appointment? This person who called?" I wait to see what happens. I don't consider the distraction as having messed up my prayer, but I include it, asking, "What kind of heart am I to have regarding this person or situation?"

Eventually, the skill of centering comes naturally and you hardly notice the noises around you. Eventually you experience times of prayer like those described by Jean-Nicholas Grou:

> Imagine a soul so closely united to God that the heart will be full of aspirations toward God without any clear expression—prostrate in God's presence and wholly lost in him.[12]

That is the joy and abandonment of centering ourselves in God. It's a goal worthy of every soul.

Notes
1. Richard Foster, *Prayer: Finding the Heart's True Home* (San Francisco: HarperSanFrancisco, 1992), p. 161.
2. Amy Carmichael, *A Very Present Help*, ed. Judith Couchman (Ann Arbor, MI: Servant Publications, 1996), p. 61.
3. Richard Foster, *Celebration of Discipline* (San Francisco: Harper & Row, 1988), pp. 30-31.
4. Jeanne Guyon, *Experiencing the Depths of Jesus Christ* (Beaumont, TX: The SeedSowers, 1975), p. 11.

5. A. W. Tozer, *The Pursuit of God* (Camp Hill, PA: Christian Publications, Inc., 1982), pp. 36, 37.

6. Henri Nouwen, *The Way of the Heart* (San Francisco: HarperSanFrancisco, 1981), p. 82.

7. Thomas Kelly, *A Testament of Devotion* (New York: Walker and Company, 1987), pp. 59-60.

8. William Law, *A Serious Call to a Holy and Devout Life,* ed. John Meister (Philadelphia, PA: The Westminister Press, 1975), p. 98.

9. "The Practice of Listening: An Interview with Madeleine L'Engle," *Cross Point*, Summer 97, p. 3.

10. Guyon, pp. 83-84.

11. Guyon, p. 71.

12. Jean-Nicholas Grou, *How to Pray* (Cambridge: James Clarke & Co., 1955), pp. 20-21.

ASKING GOD QUESTIONS

P EOPLE OFTEN SAY THEY HAVE QUESTIONS TO ASK GOD WHEN THEY get to heaven: "What causes cancer?" "How can the moon so far away create tides in the ocean right here?" "Why did you make my brother (or sister) so good-looking, and me so plain?"

Making such a list is not a silly idea, I think, because it shows we view God as someone who knows things and wants to communicate with us. Here on earth, we can cultivate such a relationship with God by continually asking God questions. We can do this throughout all of life—while taking a walk or running errands—but it's also been a fundamental element of contemplative prayer for me. Posing questions to God helps us stay alert in the silence, and it provides structure for anyone made uneasy by the open-ended nature of contemplative prayer. We offer questions in silent contemplation, and then wait. Sometimes a thought will come, but more often the answer will surprise us, coming at an odd moment later that day . . . or week or year.

ASKING

Now that we have grasped the first part of the prayer of the heart—which is surrendering ourselves to be filled with His presence—we can address the asking part of prayer in the right context.

Jesus said we could do nothing apart from Him (see John 15:5), but that does not stop us from trying. The whole point of asking, seeking, and knocking in order to inquire of God (see Matthew 7:7) is to interrupt our constant pull toward independence from Him. Without the discipline of inquiring after God, we often follow the normal human method of doing things, which is to size things up from our own perspective and make decisions on our own, with little thought of asking God's direction. Asking invites God into our situations, great and small.

"INQUIRING OF THE LORD"

Asking questions can make a dramatic difference in outcomes, as evidenced by the lives of men like Saul and David.

History shows how they responded differently to similar situations in which the Philistines had assembled against Israel. Saul, a worldly wise person, didn't ask God questions, while David sought God's counsel and remained open to it.

Admittedly, Saul's situation must have been terrifying. As Israel watched three thousand chariots, six thousand charioteers, and countless Philistine foot soldiers approach, the Israelites grew terrified. Many hid in caves, pits, and cisterns. Others fled. Saul stuck it out, while his troops quaked in fear. He'd also received a message from the prophet Samuel not to begin the battle until he arrived to perform the sacrifice to God. Saul delayed the battle for seven days, waiting for Samuel. But Samuel didn't come and the men scattered even more. So Saul did the sensible can-do thing—he offered the burnt offering himself.

At that moment, Samuel arrived, asking, "What have you done?" Saul defended his actions: "I did not want to meet the Philistines until I had sought the LORD's favor." Because of this and other offenses, Samuel prophesied that the kingdom would be ripped from Saul's hands (see 1 Samuel 13:5-15). He must have wondered what went wrong—he'd done what any sensible commander would do. Frankly, this passage is annoying for a doer, an achiever, a mover and shaker. What did God expect?

David, on the other hand, had an inquiring, reflective heart. Once again, the Philistines raided the valley, but David—now king—

inquired of God, asking if he should attack the Philistines. To a military person, this was a no-brainer decision. Attack, of course! But David asked God about each battle, knowing that God's will was not always the same, not always obvious, and is often more clever than we can imagine.

God answered David in a yes-but fashion: "Do not go straight up, but circle around them and attack them in front of the balsam trees. As soon as you hear the sound of marching in the tops of the balsam trees, move out to battle, because that will mean God has gone out in front of you to strike the Philistine army" (1 Chronicles 14:14-15). For those who believe God doesn't speak, it's startling to see that God not only speaks, but also leads an army, giving them the "go" signal in the rustling of trees (see 1 Chronicles 14:13-17). God's pattern is to go before us, and if we inquire of the Lord, we will know how to follow.

Inquiring after God about the events of our life is not a painful, drudging activity — although it might seem so to those of us who are like the commonsense, *just-do-the-job* Saul. It is a normal response for one who is pursuing God's heart. It flows out of great love and partnership with God. It becomes a complete life orientation, so it's no longer a big deal. We walk through life with hands outstretched — asking, seeking, and knocking. We become dreamers before God, asking, "What is it you are going before me to do?" We become open-hearted: "We learn to ask God to think His thoughts in us. Instead of telling God what we want from Him, we ask Him what He wants us to do."[1]

QUESTIONS WE CAN ASK

If we want to live life as an ongoing conversation with God, we will frequently ask these foundational questions:

- What are You telling me about my relationship with You?
- What are You telling me about how my character needs to change?
- What are You telling me about how You want me involved in advancing Your kingdom?

Questions sometimes come from the dilemmas of life: What do I do with this impossible situation? Why does he misunderstand me? Other times, they're general, but important: What next? What do I need to know about this person? This circumstance? As we prepare even for leisure moments, we can find some quiet and ask God, What do I need to know about this weekend? What does my hostess-friend need? What does my spouse need? What does my body need? How can I tune in to the strangers I will meet and enlarge their eyes to Your kingdom?

Sometimes we ask questions out of puzzlement. Both Mary and Nicodemus asked this important question: "How can this be?" (see Luke 1:34, John 3:9). This is the core question behind accepting the great paradoxes of God and of life. Asking this question and resting in it sets us up to recognize the answers when we hear them.

For example, I've been asking that question a lot in the last few years. As I've encountered more people than usual who have had little in this life to help them, I've asked God, "How can this be?" I have friends who were abused as children, or kidnapped and hidden by one parent for years. I've written about children in developing countries who toil long hours in mines and factories and die. I have grieved and asked God repeatedly: "How can this be?" Yet in the quiet times, when my soul was fixed on God who is Love, nothing came to me. I reminded myself of what I already knew: God is not the author of this destruction; He weeps for us in our despair. But still, *How can these things be?*

A few months ago, as I read the Gospels through, I was struck by Jesus' parable of the workers who began work at various hours of the day — some of them at the last hour, in fact — and yet they are paid equal wages (see Matthew 20:1-16). The landowner asked those he found not working at the eleventh hour: "Why have you been standing here all day long doing nothing?" They replied: "Because no one would hire us." It struck me: These were the unemployables and those lacking opportunity — much like the homeless clients at the drop-in center where I volunteer. A lot of these guys have accepted Christ, but they're still homeless. Then the connection came: These people, including an elderly Christian gentleman friend who recently shot himself in despair, have been loved by few people in this world. They were ridiculed as children. As adults, they're difficult to employ because they don't get along with people. They're eleventh-hour people, not only because some of them come to God late in life, but also because out of a "twenty-four-hour" life they had only "one hour" of being loved and valued. But this lack of opportunity on earth does not change their invitation from God into eternity. If they choose Christ, they can receive a full reward from God, and that lightens the grief in my heart. And so, an answer seemed to come to my question, *How can these things be?* God seemed to tell me, *Their persecution is not for long. I love them and will show mercy on them.*

"Hearing" that from God as I did, and knowing that God always invites me as a partner in mission, made me pray even more for the child laborers all over the world being victimized by oppressive conditions. Because God sees and God provides a full reward, I don't have to be discouraged and put them out of my mind. I can pay attention to them, contribute to works that are trying to help these people, and create an awareness of their plight.

Asking "How can this be?" in contemplative moments sets me up to "hear" my answer when reading this parable later. Technically speaking, I didn't get an answer to "How can this be?" but to "What's God doing for them?" I have a sense God is going to tell me more about this, and my continued waiting in quietness is a signal that I'm listening and receptive. So far, I don't *know* more—but I am more tied to the heart of God and more willing to use my resources to show God's love than I was before.

VESSELS OF HIS WILL

As we ask God questions in prayer, we live from the heart, always asking, "How can I be compassionate in this situation? How can I live out justice here?" We continually ask the question the rich young ruler asked: "What do I still lack?" (Matthew 19:20). His heart was divided between God and money. How is our heart divided?

We change from being "askers for things" to being "simple seekers of God." We're no longer giving God a laundry list of things to do, but asking questions about God's will. We no longer live primarily for things, but we live to have more of God in us. Bernard of Clairvaux was often called upon to help the rich and powerful of his day make loving, godly decisions. He asked, "O Lord, you are so good to the soul who seeks you, what must you be to the one who finds you?"[2]

Asking questions helps us let go of the need to fix others, the world . . . and even the prideful tendency to correct and direct God Himself. Instead, we listen carefully throughout the day, and when things happen, we ponder what question God is answering. In a relationship where someone is disrupting my life, my prayer is no longer "Make that person more sensitive." Instead, I'm asking and waiting: "What do I need to do with this unsettledness? What do I need to know about this person?" Once that becomes clearer, I can ask, "What do I need to do to show God's compassion or justice?"

As we wait for answers, a kind of "simmering process" seems to go on, and it must be allowed to do its work. I may not understand the answer until so much time has passed that I may have forgotten the exact question, but I know that I've absorbed something God wants me to know. We trust that answers will come and God will speak. Accepting this simmering process helps us to continue in faith, even when we don't know all we think we need to know. In a true sense, I no longer need to know "what" because I know the "Who" who has the ultimate answer. For many believers, Christianity is about having the answers to life's problems. To offer questions to God is to stop that obsession with knowing. We admit that we understand little of what goes on this side of heaven. It may not look as if the clouds are gathering for a storm, but I can rest because I have God's companionship, and that is enough. Decisions aren't so harrowing—because I know the light dawns slowly, but will come as needed.

WHY WE DON'T ASK

If you're like most people, you don't plan to leave God out by not inquiring. For various reasons, you just forget.

I already know. You assume you know the answer—especially if it concerns something at which you're skilled. King Saul was, after all, a tall, dynamic military leader. Sending out scouts might have seemed more strategic than asking God for direction.

I have a strong opinion about this. Let's say your spouse wants to visit someone on vacation, but you're sure you don't want to do this. You give an automatic answer without inquiring of the Lord. So often when I have inquired of God about something such as this, the result has been that I've either had a change of heart or I sympathize with my spouse and come up with an idea that satisfies both of us. The process of inquiring is important because it helps us see the other person's heart.

I like one-size-fits-all answers. The answer or solution found last time becomes a formula; every dilemma has the same answer. For example, Saul went ahead and made the sacrifice; it seemed obvious that attacking first was a good strategy because the Philistines were encamped. That was the military formula. Today, we resort to our own formulas—doing things as they've always been done, doing what's advised in the current bestseller—when we could be inquiring after God for His ideas.

Sometimes we circumvent God because we've become so policy-oriented it doesn't occur to us to stay open to God's guidance. At a retreat, some leaders asked me what I thought their church's policy should be about having baby showers for unwed pregnant women. So far, they had done nothing because giving a shower might indicate approval of premarital sex. Yet they felt bad about neglecting these young women.

I asked, "What are these women's names? What has each woman said about having a shower? What is known about the condition of each woman's heart toward God?" I then named each one and asked, "If the church had a shower for _____, what would that tell her about God?" A shower from the church might embarrass one but affirm another. Did any of them need the financial rewards of a shower? Would any of them desire, in addition to a shower, to meet with one of these female leaders on a regular basis? "Find out what these women need," I urged them, "and then get on your knees as a leadership team and listen to God together. Make it your goal to determine how God wants to use you in each woman's life." *This method is blessed, so I use it.* We often assume certain methods or people are blessed by God because they seem successful. Should I raise my kids a certain way? We think, *Sure, it worked for him,* so we don't ask God—which might cause us to look in our children's hearts and see if these methods are appropriate. Pastor and author Peter Lord writes:

> When God has blessed others by using certain methods, we sometimes presume that *we* should use those same methods. We don't realize that God blessed that way for others because that's the way he ordered them to do things. Nowhere is this more common than in church programs. One church prays and receives an answer — a specific method of carrying out a certain order of God. They are richly blessed because God blesses what God orders. Then another church, seeing this blessing, copies the program — because they believe God is blessing the program itself. They fail to realize that what he is really blessing is *obedience*. And they never stop to ask him, "Father, what do you want *us* to do?"[3]

When God gives seeking hearts a certain answer, it may not be His answer for you as well.

I've already heard God speak. Even when you've inquired of God previously and sensed His direction, schedules change, bodies change, locations are different, and bosses are different. It's important to pray and seek God continually.

ACTIVE WAITING

Asking God questions requires an extended time of waiting for an answer. While waiting is the bane of the doer's existence, consider this: Waiting on God[4] is a problem only if you're in a relationship with God for utilitarian purposes — to get the prize from the vending machine. But if you're in the relationship for God Himself, waiting means you still have what you want — God — even while you wait. It means that God, the One who turns to us and hears our cry, is paying attention (see Psalm 40:1).

Those who practice contemplative prayer get used to waiting on God in expectant alertness. Because God is liable to answer questions asked in contemplative prayer anywhere in life, we stay alert beyond the official moments of prayer. The waiting is active — being fully present to each person and circumstance, convinced that God is on the move, wanting to be there to see what happens. It is as open-ended as wordless contemplation. You don't know exactly what will come, only that God is present.

Active waiting increases your faith as you trust that more will be revealed eventually. If I wait, attentive to the inner heart, details will come. That makes it easier not to panic, but to delay trouble-some decisions without feeling indecisive. When I had to make an important decision regarding my son, I was bombarded with propa-ganda for one side. I had a hunch the other choice was better, but my son wanted the first one. During one day, people checked with me, hour by hour, to find out what my decision was. Finally, I told these people I wouldn't know until the next day.

In the quiet of that nondecision, I asked God, *What do I need to know?* As I returned to work and other aspects of my day, another question formed in me: *What are Your goals for this boy? What char-acter qualities have You been trying to build into Your son?* That was simple—he was already an accomplished achiever, but I had prayed that he would grow a tender heart for others. Then: *Which situation is filled with adults who exhibit a tender heart?* Suddenly the solu-tion was simple. I chose the group whose adult leaders exhibited the tender heart I want my son to have.

The contemplative way has taught me to pause when things are unclear and wait for clarity. When in doubt, wait. For quite some time, I'd wondered if I needed to resign a certain position, and so I worried about what I should do. But my friend wisely advised me to wait, saying, "God will show you." So I waited. Sure enough, a cri-sis of conscience arose and I knew it was time to resign. It's true that God will show you, and waiting on God helps us trust Him. I've had difficulty making decisions in the past and have wasted time worry-ing about them. Waiting for God to make it clear can be so helpful.

The skill of active waiting also helps us live through wrong deci-sions. We ask God, "How do I live from the heart, behaving with justice and mercy, in this situation I should never have gotten myself into?" One time I agreed to be a part of a conference simply because I thought it would help me promote my books. Shortly after, I saw that the philosophy of the conference differed drastically from mine and that I'd made my decision based solely on self-promotion. I had no business presenting there, and if I'd thought about it, I would have figured that out. As I languished over my poor judgment, I waited on God, asking, "What am I to do now?"

As time passed, it seemed that God was asking me to do what I always do when I speak—to have the heart of Christ, to help people hear Him. Would I go there to pray? Would I look for people whose needs I could meet? Would I stay away from self-promotion while there? Indeed, my sessions went well and I managed to have significant conversations with people who were hurting. If I hadn't asked God for input, I would have gone with a sour, critical attitude and accomplished little.

Still another advantage of active waiting is that it helps us set aside our calculating ways. At first, calculation of our advantages is innocent and helpful: "What is the best buy?" Then it becomes "When is the best time to approach someone from whom I want a positive response?" Or "How do I word my résumé so I am the chosen candidate?" Gradually, our manipulative attitudes take over until we're wondering, "How can I get out of God what I want?" We're back to using God as a vending machine.

Respite from Ourselves

If contemplation has an opposite, it must be *calculation*. The silence of contemplation and the listening habits of the contemplative lifestyle help you live from the heart so that when calculating tendencies besiege you, you set them aside. I choose not to "work the room" for the best networking contacts, but to stand back and watch for what God might urge me to do. I am given a respite from myself and all the demands I make—on me, on God, on life, and on others.

At rest from these self-centered drives, we learn to be present to God and others. Whereas in the past our selfish thoughts advised us to calculate the value of a person's worth to our cause, we learn to be present to other people regardless of their apparent position or personality. Our so-called "evangelism" is no longer an orchestrated set of questions and maneuvers but the outflow of a life that sees others through the eyes of Christ. Even when involved in something that cannot be technically classified as a witnessing situation,

I am praying for my friend, asking God to show me what is needed in my friend's life. This different type of "asking" results in a different type of life—centered on God instead of self. Asking God questions and waiting actively for His input make the following prayer by Amy Carmichael more appealing and more likely to be fulfilled:

Holy Spirit
think through me
till your ideas
are my ideas.[5]

NOTES

1. Frank C. Laubach, *Channels of Spiritual Power* (Westwood, NJ: Fleming H. Revell Company, 1954), p. 97.
2. Bernard of Clairvaux as quoted in *Weavings*, January/February 1998, p. 23 (exact source not cited).
3. Peter Lord, *Hearing God* (Grand Rapids, MI: Baker Book House, 1988), pp. 58-59.
4. Psalm 5:3; 27:14; 37:7; 38:15; 40:1; 130:5,6
5. Veronica Zundel, ed., *Eerdman's Book of Famous Prayers* (Grand Rapids, MI: William B. Eerdmans Publishing Co., 1983), p. 69.

WHAT TO EXPECT

I F YOU ARE NEW TO CONTEMPLATIVE PRAYER, YOU MAY BE WON-
dering: *What can I expect to happen when I pray this way? What
about my own thoughts? How will I know if I have a genuine
encounter with God?*

I want to explore these questions because some enter into contemplative prayer with certain expectations. For them, it's like waiting
for lit dynamite or skyrockets to go off but it never happens. The content of contemplative prayer is rarely dramatic. You will not hear
about changes of doctrine or improvements on the covenant—nothing that contradicts either the letter or the spirit of the Word of God.
In fact, what we sense from God will not only line up with the Word
of God, but make it more plain and down-to-earth to us than before.

What we can expect most of all is to be loved. Love—which is
the core of the good news—is the key feature of contemplative
prayer. You can expect to encounter a quiet sense of resting in God's
love and acceptance, *even* in times when you sense God is also correcting you in some way. John Wesley spoke of meeting God and
being "strangely warmed."[1] The repeated message in contemplative
prayer is just that—you are loved. Along with the key element of

love, there are other features you can expect to "sense" or "know" in contemplation. These may occur in extended solitude or during the quiet pauses of life. (The kinds of things God is likely to say, based on Scripture, are detailed in section four of this book.)

Expect to Be Surprised

If what you sense from God never contains anything that surprises you, you're probably making it up yourself. It is likely that God is speaking when what you hear sounds nothing like you, or when it is so simple or so profound you would never have thought of it. Wendy Wright says contemplative prayer requires that we "listen adventurously enough to be utterly surprised at what we hear."[2]

If you find you're trying to make up what you hear, you don't need to be embarrassed. It's normal to try to "make something happen," especially at first. This has been such a problem for me that I generally set aside the first thing that comes to me because it's often something birthed by my brain, not God's heart. If you're a wisdom gatherer (reading books, listening to tapes, and so on), you're bound to have stored up a lot of wise thoughts in your mind. Your mind then draws on them to imitate the Holy Spirit speaking. If that happens, set aside these brilliant ideas and keep waiting on God. Companions of God realize that God appreciates their mediocre answers but has heat and light of His own.

Expect to Hear Specifics About General Commands

Numerous examples occur in Scripture in which God gave specific instructions about general ideas. When David wanted to know God's will about fighting the Philistines, he didn't look it up in the "Law of Moses," the Scripture of his day. David inquired of the Lord, and got a detailed answer about waiting to advance until he heard God moving in the rustling balsam trees.

Much of what comes to me in contemplation are clues about how to specifically obey what I already know is right. I know I should love enemies, welcome strangers, and express truth graciously, but I haven't a clue about how to do that today regarding the woman with whom I volunteer. In contemplation, the clues come. I have experienced this many times regarding positive discipline ideas for my teenage children. I've read many helpful parenting books, but formulas don't always work. So as I pray for my children, often using that breath prayer, "Show me the heart of this child," I see each one's heart and then ideas come to me. They are always practical not theoretical, helpful not punitive. They're not dreary, but even funny at times. They're so full of grace they *can't* be my ideas.

EXPECT TO BE GIVEN UNUSUAL GRACE TO OBEY

Because contemplative prayer is a spiritual discipline, expect God to use it in your spiritual formation. Expect your heart to change and to find the grace to obey. The resentment you held tightly at the beginning of the prayer you can now lay aside. The person you criticized yesterday you *want* to encourage today. The person you were competing with you now have compassion for. It's not unusual to be praying and see the face of your coworker, or aging father, or the missing child from today's mail. In these times, God seems to be asking, "What about this person? What will you do?" You want so much to help that your heart is full.

In these moments we are strangely nurtured by the love of God to the point where we want to do God's will—to love, help, risk. This is good because many of us *know* what is right, but we struggle with *wanting* to do what is right. The more we ignore opportunities to do right, the more likely we are to become dry, brittle, law-abiding Christians who find sin quite natural. More than anything else, contemplation is about creating a space in which a change of heart can occur, and then a change in our behavior.

EXPECT TO BE EXAMINED AND FOUND LACKING

As you progress in contemplation, expect to see more of your *real self*. The echoes of past failures may appear as "barbed words spoken deliberately; thoughtless words spoken hastily; envious and prying eyes; ears that rejoice in iniquity; greedy hands, haughty looks."[3] God shows us how we have gone wrong by calling evil good, labeling darkness as light, and mistaking bitterness for sweetness (Isaiah 5:20). "So it is with all who enter into real solitude," says Elisabeth Elliot. "The layers of acquired knowledge, conditioned behavior, and self-confidence are sloughed off. The vision of self without all its accustomed accretions is shocking."[4]

Expect to hear your inner thoughts in a truer way than ever before — thoughts of greed or vengeance, self-pity or anger. The truth is that "I pretend to be better than I am"[5] and so I'm sickened to discover how I've deceived myself. I say I care about this person, but I don't. He's too rich, she's too attractive, they're too clever. Contemplation is full of self-examination: Am I jealous because I'm not the center of attention? Because that person's presence makes me wish I made more money?

"An examination is being given to you by God," writes Madame Guyon, and the best response is to embrace the examination, not to run from it. "Lay your entire soul open before God," she counsels. "You can be certain that the Lord will not fail to enlighten you concerning your sin. Your Lord *will* shine as a light in you; and through His shining, He will allow you to see the nature of all your faults."[6]

You will also see your fears in a new way. Once when traveling to speak at my alma mater, I found myself irritable the day before. I sat quietly before God, asking, "What's this about?" Yes, I was nervous about speaking before my college professors, but in the quiet I realized I was returning two weeks before the date twenty-five years earlier when a tornado had damaged the campus, our car, and our mobile home. It never occurred to me that I could be afraid of a tornado. I was a survivor of California's massive Northridge earthquake and four years of aftershocks! But there in the quiet, I admitted my fear and saw my irritability fade.

Exams generally make us nervous. But we can remain peaceful because these spiritual examinations by God are nothing like being dressed down by a teacher or criticized by a supervisor. Says Madame Guyon:

> Since it is your Lord who is [giving the examination], and no one else, you should simply remain peaceful and calm before Him as He carries out this exposing. Depend upon your Lord, not on yourself, to show you the extent of your sin. God does all the revealing.[7]

God is a safe examiner because He is the Potter, the shaper of our hearts, the One who has nothing to gain by putting us down, and He earnestly desires the transformation of our soul. In the safety of God's company, our faults aren't so demeaning. We can let down our guard and be open to what God is saying. The simplicity of the silence is rejuvenating and reassures us that God can transform doubt into trust, annoyance into calm, and fear into serenity. We can even adopt the *here-I-am* spirit of Isaiah, which brings expectancy that God will do something interesting any minute — and I want to be a part of it.

These exams become moments of sweet repentance as God's love breaks through the walls we've erected and changes our hearts, setting us up for drastic character changes. "Solitude molds self-righteous people into gentle, caring, forgiving persons who are so deeply convinced of their own great sinfulness and so fully aware of God's even greater mercy that their life itself becomes a ministry."[8] Without solitude, we remain victims of other people's opinions — governed by "he says" and "she says" rather than the still, small voice of God.

Once, I asked my friend Rosemary to give me some guidance in Christian discipleship. She mentioned that several others had asked her the same thing. She suggested that she start a group and I could help her. The first night we met, I didn't like the meeting. She sat in the brown corduroy chair in which she always sat, and I sat in the one opposite her. The four other women sat on the couch. Week after week I disliked it more. Finally, I told my husband I was going to quit. "Are you *allowed* to quit?" he asked. "You helped her start it." Then he asked me that great question I love to ask God: "What's this about?"

So I went to God in the quiet, asking, "What is this about?" Within just a few minutes, it became clear to me: I was jealous of the other women in the group. I'd really wanted Rosemary's time and attention all to myself. I knew I needed to confess this to her, and I did. Through the grace she showed me, I stayed in the group and it became a powerful force in my life as I experienced community with people so different from me.

These experiences in contemplation can permeate our lives. You get in the middle of baffling situations and ask, "What is this about?" If you've practiced this enough in contemplation, you'll be able to do it on the spot. "Once you have established such a relationship with your Lord, you will soon discover that no fault in you escapes the reproof of God. As soon as you commit a sin, you are immediately rebuked by an inward sense."[9] You quickly admit the sin to God and experience a so-glad-to-be-home sense. You learn to put away feelings of "Oh, no, not again" or "I can't believe I'm so obtuse" or "How does God put up with me?" God is a dear parent, and so instead we say, "I get it now."

Expect the Defects of Your Heart to Be Revealed

When I seek God, I'm most likely to hear about *my* faults, not *yours*. The problem occurs when we assume that with God "one size fits all"—that what God is telling me He is also telling you . . . *so listen to me, buster!* This crosses another person's spiritual boundaries. We've developed different failings along the way. God may be urging me to be more outgoing while urging you to be more private. We need to respect what God might be telling another person.

An illustration of this appears in Jessamyn West's book, *Friendly Persuasion*, in which two sons of a Quaker minister and her husband were asked by a recruiter to join the Civil War effort. The parents opposed, but the son named Joshua decided to go. As he rode off early one morning, his brother Labe caught up with him to trade horses so Josh would be equipped with the better horse. Josh apologetically explained to his brother that he had to go and fight because he was afraid to go. Labe later explained to Josh that he couldn't fight because he knew in his heart he loved fighting.[10]

In the spirit of contemplative listening that Quakers practice, both sons looked in their hearts. One found fear and the other found violence. They obeyed God with different behaviors that overcame their individual doubt and sin. They didn't base their decisions on what the town thought (fighting was right) or what their parents thought (fighting was wrong), but they looked in their hearts. They each tried to make a decision in the spirit and character of Christ, asking, "What is God calling me to overcome? What must I do to overcome it?"

Expect to Hear Your Soul's Neediness

As silence becomes a friend, we can sense our raw inadequacy and sin. We may recognize and admit the basic drives behind our inappropriate behavior. For example, we may resent others because of chronic fear, numbed anger, or fleeting self-doubt.

This neediness often surfaces as job or relationship difficulties. If we're wise, we examine them in the quietness of contemplative prayer. As we uncover these hidden motives in the soul, we find things that are difficult to admit to anyone. It may scare us as the huge gaps in our character open like crevices before us. In fact, the neediness can be so devastating that you stop praying and go wash the car. But if you keep paying attention to that fear or anger or doubt, it—and you—will be embraced by the love of God. You will understand that God shows us this because God wants to work with us.

Neediness usually develops within the following areas:

Core beliefs about yourself. Gaps in character spring from core beliefs that govern our behavior. For example, one man found through self-examination that he believed in his heart that everyone else had it better than he did. *Others* got promotions, but he did not. *Others* had been raised by loving parents, but he had not. *Others* were good-looking, but he was not. As a result, he compared himself to others and felt "less than." He resented others' successes and figured no one's struggles were as great as his. As time passed, he saw this was at the root of his resentments toward other people and even toward God. It helped to lay this before God in the quietness of prayer over and over, as healing occurred.

Core beliefs about God and self. One of the most common pains of inner neediness is our doubt that we are loved by God. This makes itself obvious when we continually seek the approval of others or try to obtain all-encompassing love from one individual—a spouse, a child, a boss, a pastor. Because this person is human and not God, this person fails, which rankles and disappoints us. Only God's love and approval is abundant enough to satisfy us. That's why knowing the character of God from Scripture is so important in preparation for contemplative prayer. God is the One who rescues us over and over (see Psalm 18), who delights in us and even sings over us (see Zephaniah 3:17), who allows nothing to separate us from His love (see Romans 8:38-39). We take these pictures back to contemplative prayer and rest in them, hearing God's words of love instead of our own words beating ourselves up. This is the knowledge of God that fuels a continuing transformation of the heart.

As you awaken to your soul's neediness, don't despair. Simply ask God what He's calling you to do. This is no small work. You will be cultivating a heart that sees yourself as you are, as Isaiah did: "'Woe to me!' I cried. 'I am ruined! For I am a man of unclean lips, and I live among a people of unclean lips, and my eyes have seen the King, the LORD Almighty'" (Isaiah 6:5).

In this solitude a seraph put a live coal on Isaiah's mouth and said, "'See, this has touched your lips; your guilt is taken away and your sin atoned for.' Then I [Isaiah] heard the voice of the LORD saying, 'Whom shall I send? And who will go for us?' And I said, 'Here am I. Send me!'" (Isaiah 6:7-8). From brokenness came cleansing and a here-I-am willingness.

EXPECT TO DO THIS POORLY

Contemplation is sometimes far from being dazzling and enlightening. Says author Madeleine L'Engle, "Sometimes I do it [silence] badly. As when I practice the piano, I sometimes practice very badly. But unless I do it every day, I can't do it well ever."[11] Doing it "badly" is not unusual and is no reason to stop. The confession of pastor and author Peter Lord lets me know I'm not alone when I do solitude poorly: "The attitude, often subconscious and unspoken, is that if God has anything to say, he had better hurry."[12] You'll get bored and you'll fall into long inner discussions with yourself: *What's wrong with her? Should I or shouldn't I go?*

At times, you'll feel as if you just don't have time. I hold on to these words from Basil Pennington, a Trappist monk who was an author and translator:

> We have all those things we want to do. We will find that when we do begin to give time regularly to contemplation, we do not lose time for other things. Indeed, we gain it. It is the experience of those who contemplate regularly, giving forty minutes or more of their day to sitting quietly in the silence, that they in fact get more done and with more peace and joy. Why? Because God has more freedom to work in their lives and they have more freedom to let God

work. They are free to not get in God's way with all their
own plans, imaginings, and fears.[13]

The time wasters in our lives are not solitude, but those "plans,
imaginings, and fears." The company of God frees us from them.

Contemplative prayer also falls short of being dazzling and enlightening when we are unable or unwilling to respond. God says to
love, but I don't want to. If I wanted to, I don't think I could. In those
situations, I often ask God, "Because I'm unable/unwilling to take
the next step in this long journey of obedience to You, what is one
small step I might attempt?"

One day on my canyon road walk, I stopped and sat by the side
of the road, despairing over my lack of desire to obey Jesus' command to love and pray for enemies (Matthew 5:44). So I offered God
the best I could. "Let's say loving this woman and praying for her is
Plan A. Plan B might be praying for her and acting in as loving ways
as possible, knowing that You will equip me to love her someday." So
I pursued Plan B (praying), and found Plan A (loving and praying)
worked itself out. To pray for this woman was the one small step I
could take that day. Eventually that prayer created compassion for
her, and then love.

WHAT IF NOTHING HAPPENS?

Suppose you manage to quiet yourself and enjoy God in wordless
prayer, but nothing comes to you—no sense of God's love, no enjoyment of God, no insights. You "hear" nothing. "Sometimes we hear
actual words in our minds and hearts when we engage in the work of
contemplation, but often the communication is wordless and yet
somehow still communication."[14] You may not realize until later that
day or the next the wordless communication you received. Often it's
a simple assurance that you're loved, assurance to move ahead, assurance that you're on the right track.

Also, keep in mind that although "nothing" happens in silent
contemplation, it may set you up to "hear" an hour, day, or week later.
Those few minutes position you as a skilled listener before God. From
this position, you become ready to hear from some unlikely source:
a child, a piece of junk mail, a coworker you don't respect.

But still, you say, "I'm not getting anything out of it. I don't sense anything." We assume this is bad only because we also assume God is in the information and inspiration business, and if no facts or feelings are perceived, nothing happens. That is not so. Thomas Merton writes: "There is no such thing as a prayer in which 'nothing is done' or 'nothing happens,' although there may well be a prayer in which nothing is perceived or felt or thought."[15]

This is not an unusual experience. "In the beginning, it is usual to feel nothing but a *cloud of unknowing*. You seem to know nothing and to feel nothing except a naked intent toward God in the depths of your being. If you strive to fix your love on God, forgetting all else, which is the work of contemplation, I am confident that God in his goodness will bring you to a deep experience of himself."[16]

If you're a person who has relied on yourself a great deal to *know* what's going on, this *unknowing* will be unnerving. As you get used to it, it will be delightful to rely on God, who is in charge and really can manage the world. You can sleep in peace tonight.

A Road Map, Please?

If the agendaless nature of contemplation bothers you a great deal, consider this bare-bones agenda suggested in the oft-quoted classic booklet by James Borst, *A Method of Contemplative Prayer*:

- Let go of thoughts, relax, and maintain silence
- Be aware of God's presence (use the image of Isaiah 6:1-8 if you wish)
- Surrender in the Spirit (use Galatians 2:20, if you wish)
- Accept others (let go of anger, resentment, and the desire to control)
- Repent and seek forgiveness (be willing to change)
- Contemplate God (listen and look for God to "show" some aspect of Himself to you)
- Receive (such as a sense of being God's "beloved"; use Zephaniah 3:17, if you wish)
- Praise (using praise psalms such as Psalms 100–104)
- Intercede (prayer for others)[17]

I included this agenda not for you to follow rigidly but to free you as you let God lead you. Scripture offers no clear road map, perhaps because prayer is not a technical, mechanical task but a relationship with God that must be learned and experienced for itself. Grou says:

> Be *simple* in your piety. Do not use so many books and exercises and methods. Let your heart tell you what you wish to say to God and say it simply without bothering too much about the words.[18]

If a skeleton agenda is helpful at the moment, so be it. As soon as you are able, though, let go of it and let God guide you.

I assure you, you can expect God to interact with you in some way and, through that, fuel your ongoing conversations with Him.

NOTES

1. *Great Devotional Classics: Selections from the Letters of John Wesley,* ed. J. Manning Potts. (Nashville, TN: The Upper Room, 1952), p. 5.
2. Wendy Wright, "Desert Listening," *Weavings,* May/June 1994, p. 7.
3. John Baillie, *A Diary of Private Prayer* (New York: Collier Books, 1977), p. 79.
4. Elisabeth Elliot, "Turning Solitude into Prayer," *Cross Point,* Summer 1997, p. 8.
5. Baillie, p. 75.
6. Jeanne Guyon, *Experiencing the Depths of Jesus Christ* (Beaumont, TX: The SeedSowers, 1975), p. 73.
7. Guyon, p. 74.
8. Henri Nouwen, *The Way of the Heart* (San Francisco: HarperSanFrancisco, 1981), p. 37.
9. Guyon, p. 74.
10. Jessamyn West, *Friendly Persuasion* (New York: Penguin Books, 1972), pp. 76-83, 100.
11. "The Practice of Listening: An Interview with Madeleine L'Engle" *Cross Point,* Summer 1997, p. 2.
12. Peter Lord, *Hearing God* (Grand Rapids, MI: Baker, 1988), p. 53.
13. Basil Pennington, "The Call to Contemplation," *Weavings,* May/June 1996, p. 36.
14. Avery Brooke, "What Is Contemplation?" *Weavings,* July/August 1992, p. 9.
15. Thomas Merton, *Thoughts in Solitude* (Boston: Shambhala, 1956), p. 46 as quoted in Timothy Jones, *The Art of Prayer: A Simple Guide* (Westminster, MD: Ballantine Books, 1997), pp. 172-173.
16. *The Cloud of Unknowing,* ed. William Johnston (New York: Doubleday, An Image Book, 1973), pp. 48-49.
17. James Borst, *A Method of Contemplative Prayer,* as quoted in Joyce Huggett, *The Joy of Listening to God* (Downers Grove, IL: InterVarsity Press, 1986), pp. 54-74.
18. Jean-Nicholas Grou, *How to Pray* (Cambridge: James Clarke & Co., 1955), pp. 47-49.

SECTION THREE

Wisdom in
Contemplation

HEARING GOD
WITH CLARITY

Think about it: "If you talk to God, it's called prayer. If God talks to you, it's called schizophrenia."[1] Why is that?

Through the years, we've been given good reason to be skeptical about people hearing God. Some have claimed to hear God and then used that "message" to tell others what to do. Some seem to begin every other sentence with "God told me." And you think, *Oh, really?*

Still, many of us have secretly wished God would speak to us. This causes us to grasp for techniques. First, we revert to seeking signs and "fleeces": "If I'm supposed to take this job, God, cause the seat of my car to be wet in the morning—the passenger side would be more convenient." "If I'm supposed to take this job, have the company offer employee discount trips to Disney World with complimentary airfare." Or we put God on a timetable: "Let me know if I'm supposed to go to this event by 3:00 P.M. tomorrow, so I have time to take my new suit to the cleaners." Or we give God multiple-choice tests: "Should I marry X, Y, or Z?"—never including the option "none of the above." Many of our attempts to get God to talk to us are laced with superstition and empty-headedness whitewashed in

God-talk.

What does it take to practice contemplative prayer in such a way that we hear God with clarity? Clearness is blocked by various snares, which we will discuss in this chapter. In the rest of this section, we'll look at other issues about contemplation that require wisdom: not letting it be pigeonholed as introversion, nor allowing it to be confined to "official" times of prayer.

PRAYING WITH A CLEAR HEART

In earlier chapters, we looked at issues that block our clarity in contemplative prayer. For example, *knowing God as He truly is in Scripture* (chapter 3) keeps us from assuming God is saying something that is outside His character. And in chapters 3 and 4 we saw how *contemplation's rootedness in Scripture* keeps us from dreaming up inappropriate "messages" from God. In the next chapter, we'll look at how *being rooted in Christian community* is also a safeguard.

These three safeguards show that past experience with God is a must. Some growth in Christ is imperative. Richard Foster says that the wordless prayer of silence "is not for the novice. It is for those who have exercised their spiritual muscles a bit and know something of the landscape of the spirit." He compares premature attempts at contemplative prayer to the way an "apprentice electrician is not allowed to do the tasks of a journeyman because he is not ready for those tasks, and for him to undertake them could, in fact, be dangerous."[2]

Why is this so? The silence of contemplation allows room for the Enemy of our soul to move in with voices that are not God's. This possibility doesn't negate the importance of contemplative prayer. If it did, we should be afraid to do any spiritual discipline, including reading Scripture. Fear of the Enemy is not God's will.

How ready must a person be for contemplative prayer? Foster notes some questions about our character that we can ask ourselves:

- Is it becoming easier to receive constructive criticism?
- Am I learning to move beyond personal offense and freely forgive those who have wronged me?[3]

At first, I couldn't figure out what the second question had to do with contemplative prayer, but then I realized that my prayer was most often disrupted by my irritable thoughts about people. As I have moved into letting go of the need to react to people, I'm brooding less over them. Ongoing forgiveness of others keeps contemplative prayer from dissolving into a struggling defeat. These questions also suggest having gotten beyond the self-absorption of always asking for things for myself. They suggest a willingness to look at our soul's inner neediness and abandon our desire to find affirmation in the opinions of others. Instead, we get our needs met in the companionship of God. If I can say yes to these questions, I'm trusting God to provide safety to protect my reputation for me.

QUIETING OUR "INNER COMMITTEE"

Some of us, it seems, have a "committee" of different selves living in our heads. Each member has an agenda and puts forth that agenda. The silence of contemplative prayer is too open an opportunity for these committee members to remain silent. Even when you shut the door on them, so to speak, they show up in full dress, pounding away. "Only when they realize that they are not welcome do they gradually stop coming."[4] Here are some typical scenes in contemplative prayer in which these committee members interrupt our times of conversation with God and make it difficult to be quiet before God.

As you sit in silence:

- a thought comes to mind about a troubled family member. The *Rescuer* in you makes it clear you ought to do something this instant to remedy the problem. Before you know it, you're consumed with problem solving.
- a quick prayer blips into your mind about an upcoming opportunity for service—chairing an event, leading a group. The *Looking-Good Kid,* the one who works hard and dazzles others with insightful comments, shows you how this service will increase others' admiration of you.
- a work situation in which you were taken advantage of pops into your head. The *Victim* mumbles about how "those people" don't treat you with the respect you deserve. Should you quit? Why do they act this way? How

could you get back at them?

- the face of someone you need to forgive appears, and before you can become attentive to that person before God, the *Defender* rehearses what exactly you could say to that person the next time you see him or her. Let's see, now, how will I ease into this clever comeback?
- a past failure comes to mind. The *Critic* reminds you of how you lack the skills and the confidence to ever be what your family or friends call successful. Why bother trying?
- nothing comes into your mind and so the *Entertainment Junkie* tells you that prayer is just too much work. Maybe you should rent a video tonight and get fixed at church tomorrow.

Not only must I set aside the voices of my committee members, but I must realize that God doesn't use them to speak to me. I cannot listen to them. They may imitate people I have loved and revered—the well-meaning but whiny, grouchy relative; the demeaning, demanding teacher—but they are not the voice of God. This is the most common pitfall in contemplative prayer. It helps to name our committee members because they represent our inner neediness yet to be healed. They sometimes echo the trends of our culture: grab more, achieve more, do something. Do you remember my telling you about Charles, king of France, scolding Joan of Arc in Shaw's play, wanting to know why she heard God and he didn't (page 85)? Imagine what the king's committee members were saying to him. Perhaps it was "Be a winner!" or "Act like a king!" or "Make that popular female military genius shut up!"

If you have this committee in your head, that's not a sign that contemplative prayer is not for you. It's just a sign you're human. Keith Miller struggled with this as he learned to listen to God. A pivotal point occurred when a friend said to him, "You've told me that you have spent many years tuned in to other stations in your mind. It may take weeks or months to be able to sort out the way God talks to you."[5]

Facing and quieting these committee members is a part of our spiritual formation. What better way to face our inner neediness than in the sweet silence of God's presence? Keith Miller's early experiences of sitting in silence listening to God every day got better:

> I began to hear things like, "Keith, you are a precious child, and I love you." I didn't know whether that came from God or just the deepest part of me. But I wept the first time I wrote it down, because I had never heard anything like that in my mind before. All the inner voices I'd listened to all my life seemed to be critical, point out faults or mistakes I had made.[6]

RECOGNIZING THE VOICE OF GOD

When we know God as He truly is in Scripture, we learn also to recognize the voice of "the thief who comes only to steal and destroy" (John 10:10). This thief's voice, unlike God's voice, threatens and intimidates on the basis of fear: *If you don't do this, you'll be sorry.* It may order you or try to force you to do things. It is often urgent and pressing, sermonizing and demeaning: *Do this now! If you wait, all will be lost!*

Jesus, the good Shepherd, however, leads the sheep but does not drive them (see John 10). He knocks at the door, He doesn't kick it in (see Revelation 3:20). God is looking for your trust in Him and an obedience of the heart, not of the panic button.

Check yourself: Do you routinely distort the voice of God with that of a negative committee member? Listen for patterns. But don't confuse these committee members with the penetrating questions and assertive, purposeful direction God gives. God may even chastise, soothe, prod, or direct. (Examples will be given in the last section.)

The simplest guide for knowing when you hear the voice of God is this: Examine what you hear, and if the command or question or comment is patient or kind, it's probably God. If it's boastful or proud or rude or self-seeking, it's probably not God. If it is easily angered or keeping track of wrongs, that could be the Enemy. You can depend on God's words to embody protection, trust, hope, and perseverance (see 1 Corinthians 13:4-8). God is not going to tell you to bomb an abortion clinic, to throw word bombs at a spouse, or to bomb a job with explosive behavior.

I wish the committee represented the only snares to contemplative prayer, but there are more. Traps of self-absorption abound. It takes ongoing vigilance not to have more faith in our own faith than faith in God.

SELF-ABSORPTION

The Cloud of Unknowing warns the one who practices contemplative prayer not to be "vainly considering [yourself] clever and sophisticated about the spiritual life."[7] You've probably met people who take on a mystical tone when they talk about prayer. Contrast that with the person who can quietly talk about God without elaboration or pious posturing.

Be careful not to dismiss pseudospirituality as a problem you will never have. It's so easy to fall in love with our own spirituality. Every once in a while I used to get the strangest thought in my head as I walked the canyon road. These walks are full of worship and prayer and that wordless delight of being before God. But then I would see myself—Jan Johnson walking her canyon road—as featured in a worship music video or on the cover of *The Los Angeles Times Magazine*.

I've concluded that there is no end to self-congratulation. Not until I confessed this little "vision" to a friend and found out he'd done the same thing was I able to let go of it and laugh about it. Recognizing our pseudospiritual tendencies can force us to make that always-healthy confession to God: "Forgive me that so much of what I do is about *me* when I want it to be about *You*."

It's possible to let spirituality spiral into self-absorption in other ways as well. It may appear as a sense of despair—"I'll never get contemplative prayer right." But it's not about getting it right; it's about being still and knowing God is God (see Psalm 46:10). Or we evaluate how we're doing with prayer—wanting longer sessions and more rapturous feelings. In this obsessive self-analysis, we run the risk of living out a paraphrase of Galatians 2:20 rather than the truth: "I have been *improved* by Christ, and Christ has made me a 'better me.'" (As opposed to "I have been crucified with Christ and I no longer live, but Christ lives in me.")

Pseudospirituality may also result in emotional frenzy. The much-experienced author of *The Cloud of Unknowing* warned against working oneself up. This is the work of the enemy, and springs from "hypocrisy, heresy and error."[8] Genuine spiritual ecstasy may occur, but if it does, you'll never see it coming, so don't plan on it or look for it. Seeking the spectacular is a sign of childishness, and holding it up for all to see is a sign that true intimacy with God is foreign to you.

TOO MUCH INTERIORITY

Let's say that as your contemplative life develops, fascination with the God you meet is replaced by an enjoyment of the interior life. It may result in "feeling holy," which, of course, is one more way to have faith in our own faith.

Joan Chittister, author of the best-selling book *Wisdom Distilled from the Daily*, tells how she discovered the danger of too much interiority in her early days in a convent training to become a nun.

The biggest shock of my early life in the community was to find out that novices were not permitted to go to chapel between the regular times for prayer. Were not permitted. Now what kind of place was this? Here I was, set to get instant holiness and impress the novice mistress at the same time, but someone apparently had figured out both motives and moved to block the whole idea. In fact, they had something much better in mind for all of us. They wanted us to work. Why?

Chittister went on to explain that pseudocontemplatives see work as an obstacle: "They want to spend their hours lounging or drifting or gazing or 'processing.' They work only to sustain themselves and even then as little as possible. They say they are seeking God in mystery, but as a matter of fact they are actually missing the presence of God in the things that give meaning to life."[9]

Solitude and reflection need to be alternated with times of exterior activity. In fact, that alternating rhythm helps us learn to practice God's presence in the mundane things of life. When I first began a time of study and contemplation on Saturday mornings, it felt so out of sync to move on to doing aerobic exercise, which I disliked at that time. Much to my surprise, God's presence was vastly evident even though my eyes were trained on the video in front of me. And then through the day as I weeded the yard, God's presence seemed as tangible to me as the earth into which I dug my fingers. During Henri Nouwen's stay in a Trappist monastery, the regimen he was given alternated times of contemplation with such things as peeling potatoes and hauling rocks from a riverbed.[10] Yet God revealed Himself to Nouwen in these work experiences. This work and prayer combination makes for a delightful experience of God.

All of these snares require that we readjust our thinking. Is our goal to know and love God? Do we want an ongoing conversation with God? We have to be determined to settle for nothing less than this. God, for His part, will always meet us.

NOTES

1. Lily Tomlin, undocumented quotation found in Dallas Willard, *In Search of Guidance: Developing a Conversational Relationship with God* (San Francisco: HarperSanFrancisco, 1993), p. 6.
2. Richard Foster, *Prayer: Finding the Heart's True Home* (San Francisco: HarperSanFrancisco, 1992), p. 156.
3. Foster, p. 157.
4. Henri Nouwen, *Making All Things New* (San Francisco: HarperSanFrancisco, 1981), pp. 72-73.
5. Keith Miller, "When God Is Silent," *Cross Point,* Summer 1997, p. 11.
6. Miller, p. 11.
7. *The Cloud of Unknowing*, ed. William Johnston (New York: Doubleday, An Image Book, 1973), p. 105.
8. *The Cloud of Unknowing*, p. 106.
9. Joan Chittister, "Work: Participation in Creation," *Weavings*, January/February 1993, p. 9.
10. Henri Nouwen, *The Genesee Diary: Report from a Trappist Monastery* (New York: Doubleday, An Image Book, 1989), throughout book, examples cited on pp. 31, 34.

CONTEMPLATIVES ARE NOT "LONERS"

P ERHAPS YOU ARE STILL HARBORING A CONCERN. YOU MAY BE thinking, *Contemplative prayer must be only for introverted, intuitive types.* With all the discussion about silence and solitude, it would be easy to write off contemplative prayer as a method for the quiet, passive temperament—reflecting until you find some sort of ethereal peace, or staring into space prayerfully.

This is not true. As Tilden Edwards says, "A contemplative is not a special kind of person; every person is a special kind of contemplative."[1]

OF WARRIOR-KINGS AND FIERY PROPHETS

Consider David, the warrior-king who was also a reflective psalm-writing shepherd. Imagine him—in contemplation one moment and killing a lion the next. Could this ancient warrior have been contemplative? It appears so. David, who also pretended to be mentally unbalanced to squirm out of a desperate situation, was schooled by God in the contemplative tradition. (See Psalms 5:3, 27:14, 37:7, 38:15, 40:1, 130:5-6.) Perhaps David even got the idea of feigning madness while waiting on God. It wouldn't surprise me, considering the practical insights I've gained from contemplative moments. For someone as practiced in solitude and contemplation as David, the border between the rich inner life and the active outer life was permeable. He must have moved in and out of contemplation all day.

Other biblical figures with significant public ministries created blocks of private moments to hear the gentle whisper of God. In Elijah's discouragement (including suicidal thoughts), the angel drew him far away geographically from the public scene for a time of resting, conversing with God, and discerning the specifics of his prophetic vision (see 1 Kings 19:12). Jacob retreated to Bethel, and God showed him his future and hope (see Genesis 31). Jesus withdrew to the desert to listen to God and began inviting the disciples to join Him (see Mark 6:31).

Still, some might write off contemplation by saying, "But I'm a Martha!"—the so-called doer in the Mary-Martha split. Or "I'm a Barnabas"—a supportive servant in the Paul-Barnabas contrast. Supposedly, Mary sat at Jesus' feet doing nothing while Martha organized the world around her. Paul wrote deeply spiritual treatises (the epistles) while Barnabas offered practical encouragement. The common thought seems to be that a truck driver, gymnast, or auctioneer would never participate in contemplative prayer. Is that true?

The traditional Mary-Martha split (contemplative versus doer) is artificial. From this one story, we've built a myth. Doers might well be doers because they draw from a well of quietness before God. For example, doer Amy Carmichael was a single missionary to India who rescued temple prostitutes, eventually establishing a home and school for them. She also wrote this:

> Give much time to quietness. For the most part we have to get our help directly from our God. We are here to help, not be helped, and we must each learn to walk with God alone and feed on His Words so as to be nourished. *Listen* and don't evade the slightest whisper of guidance that comes.[2]

The fact is, you can be a contemplative and still be very active in life. In fact, your doing is likely to be far more focused, powerful, and sustained. Both Augustine of Hippo and Bernard of Clairvaux constantly took part in politics between religious and civil authorities. Three years after entering the monastery, Bernard was sent to found the abbey at Clairvaux and served there as abbot until his death. During that time, he founded more than sixty monasteries and assisted in founding three hundred more.[3] Augustine was not only an ecclesiastical and liturgical leader, but also a magistrate, "assaulted by his congregation with small claims disputes and forced to beseech a haughty civil service on their behalf."[4] Yet in the midst of all this distracting flurry, both of these men (as their writing reveals) made seeing God and loving God a primary pursuit of their lives.

Contemplation is also not, by any means, the sole domain of deep thinkers like the apostle Paul. It requires that we learn to quiet ourselves, but it doesn't require analytical thinking. The contemplative way can be a relief for the many who perceive prayer as "hard mental work, quite fatiguing, especially if reflective thinking is not one of our strengths. Thinking about God becomes one more demanding burden [in a] culture in which high value is placed on mastering the world through the intellect. God, too, is a problem that has a solution, and by strenuous efforts of the mind we will find it."[5] The Enemy of our soul, I'm sure, wants you to believe that prayer is a difficult mental task and useless to you if you're not a scholar.

CONTEMPLATION AND COMMUNITY

We have spoken so far about contemplation as an individual discipline. But it is not always a solitary activity. Some have been surprised that my book of meditation and contemplation sessions, *Listening to God*, is for small groups as well as individuals, but *lectio divina* has been done in groups for centuries. In my experiences in group meditation and contemplation, I've found that relating what I "heard" to others deepens the experience and is part of the experience itself. As I speak aloud, things become clearer to me. The response of the person across from me—who views life differently from me—is so enlightening. Sitting in silence with a room full of people is a different kind of fellowship. I find it immensely bonding. We have cared enough for each other to be quiet together. We don't always have to be jabbering at each other to minister to each other.

Community, in fact, is important to contemplative prayer because it provides another safeguard as we share our experiences and listen for others' confirmation. "The tendency in the early Quaker movement for people to 'hear' excessive and bizarre promptings was soon tempered by the practice of *communal listening,* in which an individual prompting by the Spirit was attended to by the entire community and the authenticity of its message tested in the silence they shared."[6]

The confirming word of others is a biblical principle and can be a safeguard for us. Christ confirmed the patriarchal promises; God confirmed the gospel with signs and wonders; the Epistles were confirmed by the preaching of the disciples (see Romans 5:8, Mark 16:20, Acts 15:27). The two-or-three-witnesses principle runs through Mosaic law, Jesus' teaching, and the Epistles' instruction (see Deuteronomy 17:6, Matthew 18:16, 1 Timothy 5:19). God makes truth plain, so if you've got some wild idea of what God is "telling" you, confirm it with two or three others.

The confirmation of community is important especially when a person hears God for someone else: "God told me to tell you." This is most likely to occur, says experienced pastor Peter Lord, regarding physical illness and personal and business decisions.[7] This is usually codependent fixing with a spiritual twist. We cross others' spiritual boundaries instead of urging them to become God-seekers themselves.

Yet it does sometimes occur that God seems to speak to one person about another, notes Lord. When this happens, it's "usually a confirming word concerning something he has already told them. God is confirming through you that they heard correctly."[8]

I was involved in a situation in which a confrontation needed to occur. I kept holding forth this situation in contemplative prayer, but God never gave me ideas of what to say. (Perhaps my committee members had too many nifty ones of their own.) Instead, I sensed God saying, "Show compassion. Speak the truth in *love.*" So I turned 1 Corinthians 13:8 into a breath prayer for myself: "Always protects, always trusts, always hopes, always perseveres."

Then one morning I woke up with a brand-new idea. I was not to be the one to confront, but I should act *within* the context of the committee that was also involved. This was so different from my way of thinking that I knew it had to be wrong—or it could be God's direction. An hour later, a member of that committee called to say she thought the whole committee should do the confronting. I saw this as confirmation, we did it that way, and it went well. I would never have believed it was God's idea without the confirmation of my colleague.

Confirmation often involves repeating what we *think* we heard from God to people we trust. They often confirm for us and possibly add to it, becoming vehicles for God speaking in our lives. A spouse (who knows your penchants and foibles so well) is an apt confirmer of what God may or may not have said. Do you find yourself reluctant to ask someone else, "Does this sound like something God might say to me? Something I *need* to hear?" Just knowing I'm going to check it out with someone else and be open to their ideas keeps me from entertaining outlandish, self-centered ideas.

A form of community that has provided this safeguard for contemplatives throughout the ages is the relationship with a spiritual director, mentor, or discipling teacher. The Holy Spirit is, of course, the real director or mentor, but He often uses a frail human to help us look at "ways of noticing and inviting the Spirit's presence in and among them day by day, often through spiritual disciplines."[9] Spiritual direction, mentoring, or discipling is not like therapy, which is oriented toward managing problems. Instead, you look at spiritual formation, asking, "What is God doing in my life? Where is God in each relationship? In each event?" Our answer, of course, comes out of our times of contemplation: What has God been saying to us recently?

If you're experimenting with contemplation but don't have this form of community, tell someone you trust and who values contemplative prayer what you sense God saying to you in contemplation. As you build community with that person, he or she will become free to give you an honest response without the fear of losing you as a friend.

COMPASSION FOR PEOPLE I DON'T KNOW

Experienced contemplatives of the past and present tell us that God, through contemplation, enlarges our heart to such an extent that we care not only about those we know, but for those we don't. Gazing on God isn't done for me, myself, and I, but to love God who *so loves* this world. We come away from contemplation equipped with a heart for bringing justice and mercy to the hungry, the thirsty, the stranger, the needy, the sick, and the prisoners, even though we've never met them (see Matthew 25:35-36).

God-driven service flows out of what you hear from God, and it motivates you to answer the call of God to advance God's kingdom and be a voice for the voiceless. Ongoing conversation with God gets you involved in redemptive work. What is God doing to redeem humankind, and how can I be a part of it? Missionary Frank Laubach described it this way: "After months and years of practicing the presence of God, one feels that God is closer; His push from behind seems to be stronger and steadier, and the pull from in front seems to grow strong."[10] We have a sense of God's hand reaching back to lead us while His other hand stretches forth unseen into His will.[11]

Unfortunately, the common method has been to care for others, develop compassion fatigue, and burn out. The contemplative way is the missing ingredient in this do-gooder theology. You're not as likely to become stagnant in your service if your conversational life with God is rich. Only God can give us enough fuel. We need to allow God to continually feed us.

Jim Wallis, part of the Sojourners community that works with the poor and the gangs in Washington, D. C., says this:

> Contemplation prevents burnout. Action without reflection can easily become barren and even bitter. Without the space for self-examination and the capacity for rejuvenation, the danger of exhaustion and despair is too great. Contemplation confronts us with the questions of our identity and power. Who are we? To whom do we belong? Is there a power that is greater than ours? *Drivenness must give way to peacefulness* and anxiety to joy. Strategy grows into trust, success into obedience, planning into prayer.[12]

His insight—"drivenness must give way to peacefulness"—reassures us that those of us who are driven are not excluded from the contemplative way. It helps us seek God instead of our own goals.

Perhaps this idea of contemplation as burnout prevention explains why Mother Teresa's Sisters of Mercy, who work among the poor and dying in Calcutta, India, don't get overwhelmed. Even though they get so much important work done, "only five hours a day of their time is spent among poor. The rest is spent in prayer and meditation and things that focus them on God. Their effectiveness and ability to keep going is multiplied incredibly because of their time with God."[13]

What happens in quiet moments with God carries over into life. "True contemplatives, then, are *not* the ones who [withdraw] from the world to save their own soul, but the ones who enter into the center of the world and pray to God from there."[14] In solitude, I pray for my children and I pray for clients at the drop-in center. On site (at home, at the center), I continue to pray and end up being a loving parent or volunteer without even thinking about it.

What I receive in my private moments with God refuels me to care for the world. Many days, in the midst of church squabbles, work problems, and family misunderstandings, I would rather crawl into a corner, stay there for a year, and pray, "*My* Father." God constantly reminds me Jesus' words were "*Our* Father." I'm not alone on this planet. God fills my cup to overflowing—how can I ignore those created by the God who fills that cup?

Contemplation also enhances community because it enables us to be the kind of people who can work harmoniously with others. In contemplation, true motives come to the surface and so we make amends to those we offend. In contemplation, we can quiet the committee members in our head who find others so offensive. The result is that we can serve side by side with others without disliking them or alienating them. Contemplation turns us into patient, others-centered workers that others want to have around.

Interacting in the world—being salt and light on neighborhood committees and councils—feels okay because my "comfort level" comes not from existing within an exclusively Christian environment (church bowling league and Christian small groups only), but from my time with God. For example, I am the only Christian on the board of a local chapter of a professional organization. I hold each board member before God in contemplation, and when a bitter fight developed, I was able to love each person through caring conversations and refusing to gossip or take sides. As a result, my relationship with a board member who had once told me he didn't want to be my friend because I was "born again" changed. Recently, he offered to help me with a project, and he invited my husband and me to a special event in his life. I don't know where this and other friendships are going, except that I keep holding forth all these board members in prayer. For me, wordless contemplation works better in this instance because if I tried to verbalize my prayer, I'd be telling God exactly how He ought to change these people. Instead, I just love them in prayer and ask God to keep working.

SALT AND LIGHT . . . AND ME

In what areas are you called to be God's salt and light—on a neighborhood council, parent organization, or bowling team? Begin by bringing your associates before God and asking Him what He's doing in the heart of each one: "How am I to be a part of what You're doing? What do I need to know to be that?"

The possibility of God transforming you into a drastically different person is real—and this will be your greatest witness. Where you once could not earn enough money, you now spend your resources to help others; where you once sought a higher salary, you now seek a higher standard of integrity; where you once argued for mercy to be shown to you, you now work to see that mercy is shown to others.

This radical change is necessary because God's will is bigger than becoming a nicer person. God wants Christ to be formed in us and for our character to be transformed: "the glorious riches of this mystery, which is Christ in you, the hope of glory" (Colossians 1:27). We are to seek God and ask, "What in me needs to be changed? Who are the enemies I need to love and strangers I need to welcome? What have You called me to do in Your kingdom?"

Within such a conversational relationship with God, it's difficult for spiritual formation not to occur. The spiritual discipline of contemplation diffuses the suffocating need to control people and circumstances and melts my need to be the perfect Christian. I understand I will be different from others. Their well-intentioned advice is interesting but not prescriptive. I can take their criticism to listening prayer and wait for God's insight.

Listening to God makes us more likely to carry out His values in our culture. It leads teachers on strike to pray for reconciliation between union officials and management. It leads men and women attracted to one another to be faithful to their spouses instead. It leads comfortable middle-class people to be heartbroken over a war in Rwanda that has left millions of children traumatized from the torture and death of their parents. It leads hardworking people to use their money not to be upwardly mobile but outwardly helpful. This quiet countercultural behavior galls a society in which the norm is adversarial politics, romantic highs, self-absorption in personal life, and greedy acquisition of one more convenience. A transformed heart, hungry for God, sees the wisdom of team politics, loving faithfully, sharing resources, and living simply.

Be assured that the contemplative pray-er is *not* a reclusive mystic with no friends. In fact, out of those quiet moments with God comes a person more willing to live on the edge for God with others. And in this way you become rooted, in spiritual community, with other people whom God so loves.

NOTES

1. Tilden Edwards, *Living in the Presence: Disciplines of the Spiritual Heart* (San Francisco: Harper & Row, 1987), p. 2.
2. Amy Carmichael, *A Very Present Help*, ed. Judith Couchman (Ann Arbor, MI: Servant Publications, 1996), p. 60.
3. M. Basil Pennington, "On Loving God," *Christian Spirituality*, ed. Frank N. Magill and Ian P. McGreal (San Francisco: Harper & Row, 1988), p. 105.
4. Patricia Hampl, "The Confessions," *Los Angeles Times Book Review*, January 24, 1999, p. 6. (Also to be quoted in the preface to "The Confessions" published by Vintage Spiritual Classics.)
5. Henri Nouwen, *The Way of the Heart* (San Francisco: HarperSanFrancisco, 1981), pp. 73-74.
6. Wendy Wright, "Desert Listening," *Weavings,* May/June 1994, p. 10, italics mine.
7. Peter Lord, *Hearing God* (Grand Rapids, MI: Baker, 1988), p. 198.
8. Lord, p. 198.
9. Tilden Edwards, "The Pastor as Spiritual Guide," *Weavings,* July/August 1987, p. 8.
10. Frank Laubach, *Channels of Spiritual Power* (Westwood, NJ: Fleming H. Revell Co., 1954), p. 96.
11. Frank Laubach, *Man of Prayer, The Heritage Collection* (Syracuse, NY: Laubach Literacy International, 1990), p. 22.
12. Jim Wallis, *The Soul of Politics* (New York: Orbis Books, 1994), pp. 196, 200.
13. Jan Johnson, *Living a Purpose-Full Life* (Colorado Springs, CO: WaterBrook Press, 1999), ch. 8. Taken from a personal interview with Christine Sine after her husband, Tom, visited the Sisters in Calcutta.
14. Henri Nouwen, *The Genesee Diary: Report from a Trappist Monastery* (New York: Doubleday, An Image Book, 1989), pp. 144-145.

A CONTEMPLATIVE LIFESTYLE

W HEN CONNIE'S SON STARTED WEARING AN EARRING, SHE TOLD
her husband, "I'm going to pray his ears bleed!" He was a
good kid, but what he did irked her.

But as her prayers took on a contemplative tone—surrendering instead of managing, listening to God instead of telling God
what to do—a new attitude slowly took hold. She found that every
time she put on earrings, she said a short, *no-agenda* prayer for the
son she loved. Inwardly, she changed, and her dialogue with God
changed, too.

As you explore contemplative prayer, expect your ongoing conversation with God to change and develop. The silence and solitude
practiced in contemplation trickle into your life, creating an inner
silence and solitude that can permeate everyday activity. Thomas
Kelly described this as "relaxed listening in the depths, unworded but
habitual orientation of all one's self about Him who is the Focus."[1]

LIVING IN GOD'S PRESENCE

Times of contemplative prayer equip us to live a life of being with
God, or what Brother Lawrence called "practicing God's presence."[2]
This contemplative lifestyle allows each life circumstance to intersect

with God through prayer. Nothing escapes God. We live in union with God all day long.

Continual prayer is what Paul described when he told us to "pray without ceasing" (1 Thessalonians 5:17, KJV). This busy missionary tentmaker did this himself: *"Constantly* I remember you in my prayers *at all times"* (Romans 1:9-10); *"night and day* we pray most earnestly that we may see you again and supply what is lacking in your faith" (1 Thessalonians 3:10); "we *always* thank God for all of you, mentioning you in our prayers" (1 Thessalonians 1:2). Life can be "uninterrupted fellowship" with God.[3]

But is this practical? Can a person do this? When Jean-Nicholas Grou was asked how the prayer of the heart could possibly be continual, he replied:

> How can it fail to be so? Keep the heart in a continual state of adoration, thanksgiving, penitence for sin, and prayer for the divine assistance. Far from hindering a man in the performance of his duties, it makes them easier, far from obstructing the use of his talents, it teaches him to put them to the use for which God gave them.[4]

Tasks become easier because they aren't all mine to do. I am free to surrender this troublesome coworker, this impossible schedule, or this upcoming medical test to God one more time and see what God will say to me. Nouwen says:

> The more we train ourselves to spend time with God and him alone, the more we will discover that God is with us at all times and in all places. Then we will be able to recognize him even in the midst of a busy and active life. Our hearts become like quiet cells where God can dwell, wherever we go and whatever we do.[5]

In the Old Testament, Nehemiah the politician can be found praying in the most unusual situations, such as serving wine to a king (see Nehemiah 2:1-4). In his downward career move from eminent politician to governor of a Wild West outpost, Nehemiah conversed with God so frequently that we find him praying in nearly all of the first eight narrative chapters. No wonder he was able to say so often, "My God put it into my heart to . . . " (see 2:12, 7:5). An intense doer, Nehemiah oversaw the rebuilding of Jerusalem's walls in just fifty-two days, fending off enemies as needed. Yet all this activity was rooted in the tears he had wept touring the broken walls in the night. There in the darkness he reflected on God's message and dedicated himself to that purpose (see 2:12).

INTEGRATING CONTEMPLATION WITH LIFE

The contemplative lifestyle requires that we learn to be attentive to God in all of life. Dallas Willard explained it to me this way in an interview:

> Let's say I'm a plumber and I'm going to clean out someone's sewer. How will I do this as Jesus would do it? If you encounter difficulties with the people you're serving or with the pipe or the machinery, you never fight that battle alone. You invoke the presence of God. You expect to see something happen that is not the result of you.
>
> If you train yourself to thank God when those "coincidences" happen, you'll see them as patterns in your life. The crucial thing is to be attentive to God's hand, not to get locked into one-on-one thinking: *It's me and this pipe!* Never do that. But it takes training not to do that. A person has to train himself to think, *Now is the time to praise God for the solution that just came to me.* That's called "life in God." Training brings you to the point where you don't have to say, "I have to pay attention!" You routinely think, *This is an occasion when God is present. This is a time to pray, to praise.*[6]

During that interview, I saw myself in my *one-on-one* thinking, *It's the computer software and me. I am in this battle alone, trying to make the contact management program work on my not-so-new system. Why won't this computer cooperate?* The thought that God was present and knew something about contact management programs seemed radical.

As we learn to acknowledge God's presence in every activity, we see opportunities we would otherwise miss and assistance we would forget to thank God for. Contemplation wakes us up, so to speak, because we become drowsy with the weight of daily duties and cares, looking but not perceiving, observing but not understanding (see Matthew 13:14).

Let's look at some of those skills of being attentive to God in all of life.

Move into an inner solitude in the midst of activity. In literal solitude, we train our hearts to listen quietly to God. In the busyness of life, we can learn to cultivate this inner solitude and gain access to it whenever we need it. One way I learned this was in times when solitude wasn't available to me. As a mother of young children, I longed to get away on Saturday mornings, but could not. Instead, I stayed in my pajamas most of Saturday morning to indicate that I was not available for normal activity but I was available if family members needed me. It was difficult, but I learned to enjoy God as I gave needed attention to family members, stationed in my bedroom to pray and read and ponder.

At times, it was terrible. I would be praying one minute and irritated with someone the next. I remember asking God, "What good do these minutes of solitude do me?" But I learned to pray whether I sat in silence or my kids were asking me questions. This sort of rhythm schools us to "live from the heart" more minutes of the day. To talk to others is to also pray for them.

Don't compartmentalize life. The contemplative way is "a life of learning to live with God,"[7] not a compartmentalized life with the "spiritual" (prayer) separated from health, work, family, or service. "Prayer and life must be all of a piece."[8]

Distinctions between sacred and secular blur as everything flows out of your love for God. Let's say that someone in a neighborhood organization annoys you, so you sit in that meeting and ponder that person's heart. You may pray more in that meeting than you do at church. The task of prayer is not sacred or secular—you, the doer, are sacred and any task you do is sacred as well. A dirty restaurant plate can be washed with a prayer for those who ate from it or in disgust at having to do such lowly work. God desires to be involved in our lives—so much so that we can look back on instances and say with Jacob, "Surely the LORD is in this place—and I was not aware of it" (Genesis 28:16).

When prayer and life are integrated, it improves moments of contemplation. Difficulties in contemplative prayer (specifically, fantasies that run wild or a sense of emptiness) come from this partitioning of life, or what Thomas Merton calls "dividing the inner life from the rest of one's existence." Problems with spirituality, he said, might be cured by "a simple respect for the concrete realities of everyday life, nature, for the body, for one's work, one's friends, one's surroundings."[9]

Delay responses. We're more likely to hear God's still, small voice if we pause long enough to let anything God might say catch up with us, asking God that question, "What's this about?"

I learned this when I was challenged by someone I'd heard speak. We talked afterward and he said in a friendly way, "Why don't you consider not affirming anyone for a while?" I thought that was strange. On the way home, I argued in my head with this person, noting that I am a recovering critic and affirmation is so helpful in that "recovery." I also noted that I'd been taking spiritual gift tests for years and I always scored high in encouragement. So, was he saying I shouldn't practice my spiritual gift?

I dismissed his comment, but each time I'd start to affirm someone, I'd find myself pausing. Then I'd ask, *What's going on inside?* As time passed, I realized that my motives were mixed. On the one hand, I loved God and served God by noticing others' good points they'd overlooked. On the other hand, I wanted to be liked, to be admired, to be considered spiritually insightful, and affirming others can get you those things. This was the first of many steps in attempting to do the work of Christ with the heart of Christ. I needed to guard my heart and keep my motives pure.

From this experience, I also learned the power of the delayed response. I have to listen to the inner neediness of my soul, and that neediness makes itself heard when we abstain from something (such as food or television or work). Our inner neediness becomes quite loud in those moments and tells us to hurry up and resume what we usually do.

The contemplative calms the heart and listens. "In that spaciousness we may find God wanting to show us great and little wondrous truths that are infinitely beyond the grasp of our minds. We find that we are given a kind of knowing and belonging in our spiritual heart that is too fine for our minds to comprehend, yet profoundly substantial."[10] That "knowing and belonging" is crucial to the transformation of our souls.

Infuse your work with prayer. Work can become a place of prayerful reflection. "How can manual work be prayer? It is prayer when we not only work with our hands but also with our hearts, when our work brings us into closer relationship with God's creation and the human task of working on God's earth."[11] Work, in fact, makes fine fodder for contemplation because it can be wordless. As I clean out my car, taking out paper cups and papers spilled from my briefcase, I am recreating a nest that transports my family and me to the places we need to be. Folding a tablecloth from a much-enjoyed dinner feels like prayer to me. Repairing a child's broken toy at the drop-in center—redeeming that toy from the trash can—feels like a partnership with God.

Recognize God in the mundane. The apostle John recognized before the other disciples the stranger on the shore who told them to cast their nets one more time. So familiar was John with Jesus' ways that when the nets got heavy, he immediately concluded, *That must be Jesus talking to us!* and he told the others (see John 21:7). In the same way, we get so used to the ways of Jesus (reading the Gospels over and over helps) that we become skilled at recognizing God at work in unexpected places—the words of a child or the sparse gift of a tattered woman. Our culture would never expect to find God there, but students of Jesus are not surprised.

As we watch a sunset, rock a baby, or play a song on the compact disc player, we can worship and enjoy God. The result is that we hear God more often. "Those who have abandoned themselves to God always lead mysterious lives and receive from him exceptional and miraculous gifts by means of the most ordinary, natural and chance experiences in which there appears to be nothing unusual," writes Jean-Pierre de Caussade. "The simplest sermon, the most banal conversations, the least erudite books become the source of knowledge and wisdom to these souls by virtue of God's purpose. This is why they carefully pick up the crumbs which clever minds tread under foot, for to them everything is precious and a source of enrichment."[12]

As we recognize "exceptional and miraculous gifts," we accept life's circumstances more easily, thinking, *Pay attention. God may be in this!* "Souls who can recognize God in the most trivial, the most grievous and the most mortifying things that happen to them in their lives, honor everything equally with delight and rejoicing, and welcome with open arms what others dread and avoid."[13]

Ordinary moments are worth paying attention to because you never know what God is up to. In biblical accounts, God was imaginative in how He spoke to people, as if He tailored it to each person. God spoke to the manipulative, conniving Jacob through a wrestling angel. Sarah, the mistress of a well-to-do nomadic household, was visited by three strangers whom she was obliged to notice and even serve. Balaam, of course, was talked to by a donkey—prophets *are* different! Moses, a former prince, experienced high-drama conversations with God on the mountain. For a crowd of Judean river folks who followed the latest prophet, God tore open the heavens and sent the Spirit descending on Jesus like a dove. For the key three who would sacrifice all—Peter, James, and John—Jesus' face and clothes became wired with power and light.

God speaks to each of us in creative ways. I have a person in my life whom I consider shallow and unthinking. Over the years, however, she has said things to me that have resonated in my heart. For many years, I disregarded her even though she was never anything but nice to me. I am just now understanding how much God has used this person I've overlooked to shape me with ideas that seemed too simple and phrases that seemed too cliché. I am so humbled that God would use her to speak to me.

Our job, then, is to pay attention to the various avenues through which God might speak. Elizabeth Barrett Browning pointed this out: "Earth's crammed with heaven and every common bush afire with God, but only he who sees takes off his shoes. The rest sit around it and pluck blackberries."[14] How often I've plucked blackberries, complaining about circumstances and people when my job was to take off my shoes, gaze at the fiery bush, and interact with God there.

Use your key phrases. The words and phrases we use to center ourselves in contemplative prayer can help us connect with God throughout the day. After a friend told me of how she got through the first hours and days after a terrible auto accident saying only the Jesus Prayer, "Lord Jesus Christ, have mercy on me, a sinner," I was inspired. It was during the El Niño downpours of the spring of 1998, and I was terrified in my car most of the time, having to drive a freeway narrowed by a mountain pass to get anywhere. Eventually, I could not get into a car without my whole body locking up. After driving even a short while, I could barely walk. On rainy nights, I pulled off the freeway and quaked with fear. Then I'd start again, repeating the Jesus Prayer and centering myself as best I could while straining to see car headlights through the layer of water on my windshield. I'd always thought "the Jesus Prayer" was some vain repetition, but every word of that prayer has taken on great meaning for me now.

A life attentive to God helps us "live from the heart," being open to God.

Describing this, Tilden Edwards says:

> I feel a certain childlike simplicity when I'm in touch with my spiritual heart. Like a cared-for child, I feel trusting of a mysterious yet intimate Presence that bears me moment by moment. Rather than experiencing complex, striving, calculating ambition and fear, I feel a certain willingness to be as [I am] and where I am. I accept the humility of not knowing very much because I want to be open for more of God's immediately guiding knowledge.[15]

Contemplative prayer, then, permeates all of life. The Western mind tends to compartmentalize spirituality, but this limits God. Our spiritual life is not one slice in a loaf of bread with other slices representing family, work, church, neighborhood, and so on. Our life with God is the leaven permeating the entire loaf. And when we ignore God's presence in all of life, our soul weakens and we shrink from being all we were created to be.

Perhaps you began this book thinking the life of a contemplative must be reclusive and passive. Now you know it's not. Contemplative living is the normal life of the believer who wants to live in the presence of God. And so it is the life of the computer technician, the salesperson, the at-home mother, and the college student who want to live directed by the clear voice of God.

It is the life of inner strength.

It is the life of peace.

It is the life that can withstand correction.

It is the life that knows it is well guided.

And that's because it is the life lived in a growing, intimate communion with God.

My prayer, as we move into the final section, is that you will settle for nothing less.

NOTES

1. Thomas Kelly, *A Testament of Devotion* (New York: Walker and Company, 1987), p. 60.
2. Brother Lawrence, *The Practice of the Presence of God* (Old Tappan, NJ: Fleming H. Revell, 1958).
3. Jeanne Guyon, *Experiencing the Depths of Jesus Christ* (Beaumont, TX: The SeedSowers, 1975), p. 3.
4. Jean-Nicholas Grou, *How to Pray,* trans. Joseph Dalby (Cambridge, England: James Clarke & Co., 1982), pp. 80-82, 85.
5. Henri Nouwen, *Making All Things New* (San Francisco: HarperSanFrancisco, 1981), pp. 79-80.
6. Original notes for Jan Johnson, "Apprentice to the Master," an interview with Dallas Willard, *Discipleship Journal,* September/October 1998, pp. 24-28.
7. John Mogabgab, "Introduction," *Weavings,* July/August 1992, p. 2.
8. Roberta Bondi, "The Paradox of Prayer," *Weavings,* March/April 1989, p. 13.
9. Thomas Merton, *Contemplative Prayer* (New York: Doubleday, An Image Book, 1996), pp. 38, 39.
10. Tilden Edwards, "Living the Day from the Heart," *Weavings,* July/August 1992, p. 37.
11. Henri Nouwen, *The Genesee Diary: Report from a Trappist Monastery* (New York: Doubleday, An Image Book, 1989), p. 147.
12. Jean-Pierre de Caussade, *The Sacrament of the Present Moment* (San Francisco: Harper & Row, 1982) p. 80.
13. de Caussade, p. 63.
14. Elizabeth Barrett Browning, in "Aurora Leigh" VII, line 820, *The Poetical Works of Elizabeth Barrett Browning* (Boston: Houghton Mifflin Co., 1974), p. 372.
15. Edwards, pp. 32-33.

SECTION FOUR

What You're Likely
to Hear God Say
in Contemplation

CHAPTER
13

GOD REVEALS
BASIC TRUTHS

Perhaps by now you've become more open to hearing God, yet you're still wondering how to keep from going off-track. That's a wise caution. Some people claim to hear all kinds of outlandish things from God. Others get stuck hearing only certain things from God—either criticism and threats, or reminders to work harder, or sweet, comforting words with no edge to them.

The best way to stay on track spiritually is to understand that God is likely to say to us what He has said before to people in Scripture. God's messages as expressed in broad themes of Scripture have not changed; He is anxious for us to absorb these truths. We have a wealth of examples in Scripture from the glory of Mount Tabor (the Transfiguration of Jesus) to the misery of Gethsemane (the night of Jesus' betrayal).

In this last section, we're going to explore the kinds of things God has said in the past and that you are likely to hear. You might even use these passages in meditation to ensure your times of contemplation are full of God's messages. Within these kinds of things God is likely to say, we listen for Him to speak to our individual heart for the formation of our soul.

In this first chapter of the section, we'll look at God's basic messages to us. We need to hear these at the beginning of our walk with God, but we never grow out of our need for them. We come back to these simple messages over and over:

- God tells us who we are: we are loved; we are valued.
- God reminds us of the big picture and of His purposes.
- God comforts us.
- God nudges us forward into ministry.

Let's look at each of these.

GOD TELLS US WHO WE ARE

We are loved. One of the first Scripture verses many Christians learn, John 3:16, talks about the world that God *so loves.* This message—I am someone God *so loves*—is a message we're likely to hear from God in contemplation. It's not a love that God manages to eke out now and then when we behave ourselves but a love that God *lavishes* on us: "How great is the love the Father has lavished on us, that we should be called children of God! And that is what we are" (1 John 3:1).

Bosses, friends, and family members may indicate otherwise, but God—the only One who will never forsake us or leave us—tells us we are loved. God is so anxious to tell us this that the only time God is pictured in a hurry in Scripture is when the father ran down the trail to the prodigal son, "threw his arms around him and kissed him" (Luke 15:20,24). Henri Nouwen describes God's father-heart in this way:

> God is looking into the distance for me, trying to find me, and longing to bring me home. In the three parables Jesus told to explain why he ate with sinners, he put the emphasis on God's initiative. God is the shepherd who goes looking for his lost sheep. God is the woman who lights a lamp, sweeps out the house, and searches everywhere for her lost coin until she has found it. God is the father who watches and waits for his children, runs out to

meet them, embraces them, pleads with them, begs and urges them to come home.[1]

Most days, however, I resemble the self-centered, self-righteous older brother more than the younger one. I haven't committed public sins—after all, I've been going to Bible study regularly—so I wonder, *Where are the good things I deserve, O God, because I'm so good?* If I had been the father in this story Jesus made up, I'd have told the servant to lock the door and let that older son enjoy a night outside. But the father in Jesus' story went out to the offended know-it-all and said, "My son, you are always with me, and everything I have is yours" (Luke 15:31). These are the kinds of words we can expect to hear from God.

We are valued. The two questions knit most deeply in our souls are these: What must I do to be loved? What must I do to be valued? "When these questions are not answered, we find ourselves searching. We may struggle to be close to people, but we can't. We may want to make circumstances work in our favor, but we can't. We may want help from God, but we can't seem to get it. We may even feel as if other Christians know some secret formula that we don't know."[2]

The good news is that the search for significance is over. We are loved and valued by God. In partnership with God, we have the capacity to make a huge difference in this world. God told us so in this picture: "You are the light of the world, the salt of the earth" (Matthew 5:13-14). The people to whom Jesus originally said this were not the elite or clever, but those who "were ill with various diseases, those suffering severe pain, the demon-possessed, those having seizures, and the paralyzed" (Matthew 4:24).

Even in our fallenness, we are the light of the world and the salt of the earth. Our striving for attention and recognition can be over as God speaks to us. "Prayer, especially meditation and contemplative prayer, is not so much a way to find God as a way of resting in him whom we have found, who loves us, who is near to us, who comes to us to draw us to himself."[3]

When I was teaching creative writing at a private junior high school, our family went through some tough economic times. Backing out of the school parking lot one day, I saw my trendy urban students staring at my car. To save money, we had sold our near-new car and replaced it with a thirty-year-old Plymouth that had been wrecked on one side and smudged with yellow paint on the other. Apparently, my students had seen me climb in the passenger side (the only door that worked) and scoot behind the wheel. I thought, *How pathetic I must look! I'm glad they can't see the push-button gears.*

As I shifted (actually, punched) into "drive," I looked in the rearview mirror and saw my reflection. I don't know if the voice was audible to others, but I "heard" it: *You are loved. You are valued. I will use you in these kids' lives.* Every day after that, I paused to adjust that mirror and review those desperately needed messages.

GOD REMINDS US OF THE BIG PICTURE

God does not shrink from reminding us of promises and truths He has already made plain. The ongoing discussions between God and Abraham illustrate this as they discussed the covenant over and over (see Genesis 12:1-3,7; 13:14-17; 15:1-6,7-21; 17:1-22; 18:1-19; 21:1-7; 22:16-18). These discussions might appear repetitive to us, but they didn't seem to get stale to the two involved. In fact, when it was presented the *umpteenth* time, Sarah was so startled she laughed. God kept reminding them, as if to say, "Do you remember what we talked about? Do you remember what I've called you to do?"

One of those reminders came after Lot chose the better portion of land and Abraham got the rest. In this moment when things may have looked bleak to Abraham, God brought up the covenant: "Lift up your eyes from where you are and look north and south, east and west. All the land that you see I will give to you and your offspring forever" (Genesis 13:14-15).

Sometimes God reminds us of big-picture concepts He has given us before by showing us an old truth in a new way. It's as if God says to us as He said to Abraham, "Lift up your eyes. You're looking at it. Do you see it?"

Expect God to bring up big-picture scriptural concepts such as redemption, reconciliation, inviting others to the kingdom, or building relationships instead of division. We get upset about doctrinal details and complicated church decisions and forget that the point is to love, to redeem, to reconcile.

The better we know God, the more our hearts beat in the rhythm of the heart of God—redemption and reconciliation. We begin "communicating with God not only about the matters of our heart, but also the matters of God's heart."[4] This is a sign of progress, indicating that we've gotten beyond prayer that is about only what *we* want, what *we* think is right, what *we* prescribe for the world. We've moved into seeking the heart of God and wanting His will done on earth.

When I was a member of a church in which an upcoming vote would decide the church's future, I begged God to tell me how to vote. I sat quietly before God, but no "answer" came. All I seemed to hear was "Don't forget to love." So I would say, "And?"

I purposed not to panic for an answer I could explain eloquently so I could join one "side" or the other. Continually, the same thought came: *Don't forget to love.* I began to see that, kingdomwise, the choice made by the vote might not be as important as whether we as Christians would choose to love each other in the process.

So I asked God to show me how I could be a force of love in a situation that became very bitter. As people quit speaking to each other, I remained friendly with everyone. Besides avoiding gossip, when given a platform or asked for my opinion, I simply restated what the Holy Spirit kept impressing on me during prayer: "God's will is to love each other—in conversations on the telephone and standing in the church parking lot."

Eventually, my decision on the vote become known and many people I loved stopped speaking to me. One time as I sat in wordless contemplation holding forth these people, I saw a picture of sheet music in my mind. I opened my eyes and "The Old, Rugged Cross" (a hymn I had not sung for years) popped into my head. When the arguing began during the vote, I walked forward uninvited and began playing that hymn on the piano. No one knew I could play, which added to the quieting effect. A man who hadn't spoken to me in days came and sat on the piano bench and thanked me. I told him I loved him, and I kept playing.

This was not me. By nature, I am a know-it-all, not a peacemaker, and so I would never have stepped out in love except that God kept showing me that the most important message was so basic: *Don't forget to love.* In this situation, many people earnestly wanted to know the details of God's will (how to vote) but forgot that God's will, most of all, was that we love each other no matter what.

In times of decision making, people often seek God in ways they have not before. But they want to obtain from God a red or green light—a quick vending-machine answer—when God is out to nurture us and form our character. We want God to give us an answer: "Go" or "Stay." But we're more likely to hear *how* we should go or stay—with compassion or integrity in thoughts and actions. Wherever I am, I work within God's great purposes: How can I work to redeem people? How can I reconcile people? How can I advance the kingdom of God? Contemplation isn't so much about answers as it is a way to be in the world.

GOD COMFORTS US

Don't be surprised if comforting thoughts come to you when you're numb with dread or taking a deep breath as you go into a pivotal meeting. Here's what you're apt to hear from God:

Don't be afraid. When Hagar and Ishmael were abandoned, "God heard the boy crying, and the angel of God called to Hagar from heaven and said to her, 'What is the matter, Hagar? Do not be afraid; God has heard the boy crying as he lies there'" (Genesis 21:17). God hears us crying. God hears our children crying. God takes away our fear as we learn to trust Him.

I am with you. I won't leave you. In the middle of that burning bush scene in which God challenged a reluctant Moses, He also comforted him: "I will be with you. And this will be the sign to you that it is I who have sent you: When you have brought the people out of Egypt, you will worship God on this mountain" (Exodus 3:12).

Thy rod and thy staff, they comfort me. In fearful situations, the Shepherd is present with His helpful tools in hand (see Psalm 23:4). As an extension of the owner's right arm, the "rod" was a symbol of power and authority; it was also defense against coyotes, wolves, or cougars.[5] In our fear, it's calming to imagine the rod in the Shepherd's skillful hands, ready for use to drive off predators.

Keep going. The psalmist feared doing God's will in the midst of trouble and anger: "Though I walk in the midst of trouble, you preserve my life; you stretch out your hand against the anger of my foes, with your right hand you save me. The LORD will fulfill his purpose for me; your love, O LORD, endures forever—do not abandon the works of your hands" (Psalm 138:7-8). God's comfort is available, equipping us to behave with integrity.

I am afraid of many things, especially economic insecurity. During layoffs and downturns, I gather up every single penny I can find—at anyone's expense. I have found it soothing that after God's command not to love money come words of comfort: "Keep your lives free from the love of money and be content with what you have, because God has said, 'Never will I leave you; never will I forsake you'" (Hebrews 13:5). I can gather up pennies, but I can also share some of them. "When Thou callest me to go through the dark valley, let me not persuade myself that I know a way round."[6]

GOD NUDGES US FORWARD INTO MINISTRY

As Moses learned at the burning bush, God isn't one to stop drawing us into ministry. One of those big-picture concepts God is interested in is advancing the kingdom here on earth, and He wants us to be interested in it too. God's will is about forward movement, and He wants us to join Him in those actions. Here are some examples of forward movement in Scripture that might speak to you:

- *Let's create some new thing.* "And God said, 'Let there be light,' and there was light" (Genesis 1:3).
- *Do good things with what I've given you.* "God blessed them and said, 'Be fruitful and increase in number and fill the water in the seas, and let the birds increase on the earth'" (Genesis 1:22).
- *Move from this place of inactivity.* God spoke through Moses to the Israelites, saying, "You have stayed long enough at this mountain. Break camp and advance. See, I have given you this land. Go in and take possession of the land that the LORD swore he would give to your fathers— to Abraham, Isaac and Jacob—and to their descendants after them" (Deuteronomy 1:6-8). To Gideon, God said, "Go in the strength you have and save Israel out of Midian's hand. Am I not sending you?" (Judges 6:14).

- *Do the tough thing—follow Me.* God challenged Abraham to leave his home and what he knew: "'Leave your country and your people,' God said, 'and go to the land I will show you'" (Acts 7:3). Jesus called the disciples to do the tough thing of following Him, leaving property and family behind (see Matthew 19:29).
- *Bring light to this dark situation.* "God, who said, 'Let light shine out of darkness,' makes Christ's light shine in our hearts" (2 Corinthians 4:6). Jesus constantly infused light into the lives of broken, outcast people whom others shunned.

In contemplation, we find a sense of partnering with God. Moses understood this, so when God said, "I have come down to rescue them" (Exodus 3:8), Moses didn't wonder, *So why am I needed?* God did the work and Moses was the vessel of that work. In the same way, God goes before us just as He preceded the Israelite armies from the balsam trees (see 1 Chronicles 14:15), so we catch up to see what God has already done before we became involved.

Still, it's scary. A friend who is a recovering alcoholic called me one day overwhelmed. She had just had a dream. "I was in a runaway chariot. It was going too fast," she told me. "My hair was flying straight back and my face hurt from the dirt flying in the air. But Jesus was holding the reins and I just hung on." I'm glad she told me that story because when God urges me to press on, I imagine myself squinting at the road ahead, my hair flying straight back and God holding the reins.

All of these messages are so basic, yet we forget them. I can be puzzled or muddling over something for days, and then in quiet moments before God, one of these basic messages comes to me. I think, *Oh . . . how did I miss this?* I feel so silly for having forgotten. But then God is so good to remind me.

To experience God and know His purposes for us—these are gifts that come to us through contemplative living. And yet there are other gifts—gifts that come in "darker wrappings," so to speak.

Let's turn our attention now to those other gifts we may expect to receive from God as our souls mature.

NOTES

1. Henri J. M. Nouwen, *The Return of the Prodigal Son* (New York: Doubleday, An Image Book, 1994), p. 106.
2. Jan Johnson, *Healing Hurts That Sabotage the Soul* (Wheaton, IL: Victor Books, 1995), p. 29.
3. Thomas Merton, *Contemplative Prayer* (New York: Doubleday, An Image Book, 1996), p. 29.
4. Luther E. Smith, Jr., "Praying Beyond the Boundaries of the Heart," *Weavings,* September/October 1995, p. 33.
5. Phillip Keller, *A Shepherd Looks at Psalm 23* (Grand Rapids, MI: Zondervan, 1970), p. 93.
6. John Baillie, *A Diary of Private Prayer* (New York: Collier Books, 1977), p. 85.

GOD REVEALS
DIFFICULT TRUTHS

I ONCE HEARD A SPEAKER SAY, "SOME CHRISTIANS WOULD PREFER TO sit curled up in God's lap for the rest of their lives. But God has other things to say to us besides, 'I love you.'"

I thought, *I know that.* But I wondered just how open I was to hear the wide range of things God might say to me. This could include confrontations, challenges, tests. In this chapter we will look at those three difficult sorts of messages, which we are just as likely to hear from God.

GOD CONFRONTS US

"Have you ever heard the Master say something very difficult to you? If you haven't, I question whether you have ever heard Him say anything at all,"[1] says Oswald Chambers. At first, that statement shocked me because I'd spent so much time battling negative images of God and coming to see God as a loving parent.

In an authentic relationship with God, we trust God enough to let Him probe us. In fact, God purposes to disturb us. We know this because Jesus told disturbing, shocking stories to awaken people from their self-satisfied spiritual lull.

We've heard the parables so often that we forget how shocking they must have been to Jesus' listeners. His stories were probably much like author Flannery O'Connor's stories in modern times. She seems to have purposely followed Jesus' method, telling stories that disturb instead of entertain. Her story "The River," for example, is about a boy who was told that he would go to the kingdom of Christ when he was baptized. Disappointed that he was yanked out of the water before he could go to the kingdom (all he'd seen was muddy water), he went back later to baptize himself and find the kingdom of Christ in the river. As he drowned, he "knew he was getting somewhere, all his fury and his fear left him."[2] I, like many readers, was appalled, thinking, *This boy died wanting to find the kingdom of Christ!* Am I that sincere and simple in my desire to see God's kingdom?

Consider how Jesus' listeners must have been appalled at first by His stories:

- A son says to his father, "Let's pretend you're dead and I'll take half my inheritance" (Luke 15:11-12).
- Employees repeatedly kill the owner's couriers (see Matthew 21:33-44).
- A homeowner knowingly builds his house on shifting landscape (see Matthew 7:24-27). (No doubt Jesus foresaw how readers in the Pacific Rim might be disturbed.)
- A rancher runs off and abandons ninety-nine sheep in the open country to find one lost one (see Luke 15:4-7).
- An employer pays all employees the same wages whether they worked one hour or one day (see Matthew 20:1-16).
- God kills off a man because he prospered and protected that investment for himself (see Luke 12:16-21).
- A man saves the life of his enemy (see Luke 10:30-37).

Yes, Jesus was the kindest, fairest person who ever lived—*and* He was also confrontive at every turn. His appalling stories exposed His listeners' inner neediness and questioned their wrong assumptions. Are we open to the confrontations Jesus plunked down to others, especially to the Pharisees, whom we often resemble?

In a mature relationship, people can stand to hear the truth. Here are some confrontations you can expect to hear from God, illustrated by scriptural examples:

This is My will, but you aren't the one I'm calling—help that other person instead. God told King David: "You are not to build a house for my Name, because you are a warrior and have shed blood" (1 Chronicles 28:3). (I always marvel that David didn't say, "But I was *Your* warrior, wasn't I?") Perhaps you want to start a new ministry—is God calling you to spearhead it or to help someone else?

Nothing works when you pull away from Me. God confronted Israel (through Zechariah): "Why do you disobey the LORD's commands? You will not prosper. Because you have forsaken the LORD, he has forsaken you" (2 Chronicles 24:20). This resonates with the theme of the poem "The Hound of Heaven," in which the poet is chased persistently by God. He flees into human love and nature, but nothing works for him. He can hear God's footsteps and God's voice speaking as he runs:

> From those strong Feet that followed, followed after
> But with unhurrying chase,
> And unperturbed pace,
> Deliberate speed, majestic instancy,
> They beat—and a Voice beat
> More instant than the Feet—
> "All things betray thee, who betrayest Me."[3]

When life "betrays" you and nothing works, this is sometimes God saying, "Nothing works when you pull away from Me."

You disobeyed and here's the consequence. In Jesus' story about a foolish, rich farmer, Jesus put these words in God's mouth: "You fool! This very night your life will be demanded from you. Then who will get what you have prepared for yourself?" (Luke 12:20). To the serpent in Eden, God said, "Because you have done this, 'Cursed are you above all the livestock and all the wild animals! You will crawl on your belly and you will eat dust all the days of your life'" (Genesis 3:14).

You could have been my vessel. God confronts sins of omission as well as sins of commission. It's as if God says, "You didn't do what I've trained you to do." The last time King Saul offered sacrifices instead of obeying God's voice, Samuel confronted him about his omissions and rebellion: "To obey is better than sacrifice, and to heed is better than the fat of rams. The LORD has torn the kingdom of Israel from you today and has given it to one of your neighbors—to one better than you" (1 Samuel 15:22,28). Saul missed out on fulfilling great potential as king of Israel because he didn't listen to God.

Stop sinning! To many whom Jesus healed, He said such things as "Your sins are forgiven," but to a lame man who had sat by the Bethesda pool for thirty-eight years, it was different. Jesus healed him and then found him in the temple and said, "Stop sinning or something worse may happen to you" (John 5:14). Was the cured man still panhandling? Was he basking in the glory of being healed? We're not sure, except that Jesus was blunt in His confrontation: Stop sinning. Sometimes the voice of God we hear is that simple.

You're not growing in spirit. Using Paul's words, God confronted the Corinthians: "I could not address you as spiritual but as worldly— mere infants in Christ. I gave you milk, not solid food, for you were not yet ready for it. Indeed, you are still not ready. You are still worldly. For since there is jealousy and quarreling among you, are you not worldly? Are you not acting like mere men?" (1 Corinthians 3:1-3).

Sometimes God's confrontations come in the milder form of questions. Once again, trust is required. Can we hear such confrontations knowing God wants to help us, not harm us? If so, they can become an important part of our conversational life with God.

What have you done? God confronted Eve with "What is this you have done?" when she had eaten from the Tree of the Knowledge of Good and Evil (Genesis 3:13). As Hagar ran away from Sarah, God said, "Hagar, servant of Sarai, where have you come from, and where are you going?" (Genesis 16:8). At times, I need to look at my behavior honestly and examine what I have done and to what dark place I am headed.

Do you see what you've been doing? God showed Jonah how uncaring and bigoted his behavior had been toward Nineveh by providing a vine that withered. He asked Jonah, "Do you have a right to be angry about the vine [withering]?" If Jonah could be concerned about a vine, "Should I not be concerned about that great city?" God asked (Jonah 4:9,11).

In contemplation, we too hear God's voice confronting us — you could have said a kind word, you could have offered to stay, you could have written a check. God often confronts us when we least expect it, and if we trust God enough, we can be willing to hear Nathan's words — "You are the one!" (2 Samuel 12:7).

While using a book to meditate on Scripture, I came to a passage that I felt was too familiar and worn to possibly glean much from, but I meditated on it anyway. As I read 1 Corinthians 12:14-26 about the church, I tried not to think, *Yeah, yeah, the body life concept. I know this.*

During the contemplation portion of *lectio divina,* the face of a woman at our church appeared behind the words "You have no need of me." I quickly answered with "Who would? She's grouchy and critical and gossipy. No, I don't need her!" I sat in those words and in the memory of that woman's face. In a few minutes I defended myself to God, "I've never told her, 'I don't need you!'" After a few minutes, I knew the response: "But she knows it anyway."

My repentance began. "What does she need from me?" I asked. Silence. Waiting. "Your attention." Oh, boy. *How,* I wondered, *could I give attention without it hurting too much?* Then, during the prayer portion of the *lectio* session, I asked God to help me hug her from behind each Sunday during the greeting time. (She complained when people gave her front-facing hugs.) As time passed, I managed to do that about half the time.

Months later, when her views were being put down by a much-admired person, I found myself explaining why her views might be good ideas. She looked at me with gratefulness and relief. Later, she even hugged me — face-to-face! I still have a long way to go before I can "need" her, but God is teaching me to love her in some fashion.

GOD CHALLENGES US

Long before God confronts us, God challenges us over and over. We don't always hear the Shepherd's penetrating challenges or respond to them, but when we do, we're likely to hear such things as the following:

Give up your obsession. Jesus challenged the rich young know-it-all as He "looked at him and loved him": " 'One thing you lack,' [Jesus] said. 'Go, sell everything you have and give to the poor, and you will have treasure in heaven. Then come, follow me'" (Mark 10:21; see verses 17-23). God's challenges are easier to accept as we receive His penetrating, yet loving gaze.

If we accept His challenges, they will make an enormous difference in our life. They will nudge us into surrendering what is most dear to us—possessions, admiration, achievements, income. We can picture God looking at us and loving us and then challenging us to stop spending money, fixing others, impressing others, having to be up front, having to be in charge, controlling a relationship, and running over people with our words or good deeds. It's as if God says, "This habit is one more thing that obscures Me—when will you give it up?"

Make a choice now—no more waiting. Through His servant Joshua, God confronted the Israelites: "Now fear the LORD and serve him with all faithfulness. Throw away the gods your forefathers worshipped. *Choose for yourselves this day* whom you will serve" (Joshua 24:14-15, italics mine). It's as if God says to us, "You have rambled long enough. Make a decision."

Yes, you've gotten in a mess with people who don't abide with Me, but behave as you know I want you to. Balaam experienced this admonition when, after beating his donkey, the angel of the Lord appeared in the road with a drawn sword, saying, among other things: "I have come here to oppose you because your path is a reckless one before me" (Numbers 22:32). Technically, Balaam had done nothing wrong *yet.* He only refused to draw back from wrong. God's urgent confrontation seemed to be: *Work through this mess by imitating Me and keeping your nose clean!*

This is your moment in the kingdom! Protective Mordecai instructed young Esther to keep her heritage a secret until the moment when it would be most dangerous to her—after anti-Semitic laws had been passed. Then Mordecai challenged her: "Do not think that because you are in the king's house you alone of all the Jews will escape. For if you remain silent at this time, relief and deliverance for the Jews will arise from another place, but you and your father's family will perish. And who knows but that you have come to royal position for such a time as this?" (Esther 4:13-14). Mordecai's appeal was not for the sake of the Jews only. He believed relief and deliverance would come anyway. His appeal was also part of Esther's spiritual formation. Would she see her purpose, come forward, and act?

Act like the person I believe you to be. Paul wrote to Philemon about his runaway slave, Onesimus, admitting that Philemon had been wronged but challenging Philemon to do the loving thing. Paul appealed to this powerful man on several fronts, then finally said: "So if you consider me a partner, welcome him as you would welcome me" (verse 17). What a challenge to be considered Paul's partner! What a challenge to be asked to forgive and accept a law-breaker! God often says to us, "Others may do this or that, but what is the natural and normal thing that one who loves Me would do? Examine what you're doing in light of Me, not others."

At the last minute, I was asked to lead a time of meditation at an event that was so politically charged that I'd spent the previous night out under the stars pleading with God to give me a good heart. I'd wanted so much to present my husband's side of the story to a few people there and rescue the situation, as only a wife knows how! I led them through Matthew 20:20-28, in which James, John (the "Sons of Thunder"), and their mother (Mama Thunder) beg for special positions. I urged the participants to examine Jesus' two questions: What is it you want? Can you drink the cup I am going to drink?

I sent them out to do the meditation and collapsed exhausted from the tension. Sitting on the floor, I picked up my handout. I re-read the passage and answering the first question was easy: "What is it you want?" For my husband to be noticed and respected as he should be. But the second question caused me to roll over and lie prostrate on the floor: "Can you drink the cup I am going to drink?" No, I pounded the floor and told God. No, I will not give up power, I will not give up status, I will not let people think less of me. Again, "Can you drink the cup I am going to drink?" I thought about Mama Thunder and turned the pages of the New Testament to find out if she had watched the crucifixion with Mary. Yes, she had (see Matthew 27:56). So could I. I would not rescue; I would drink the cup of suffering that Jesus (and Mama Thunder) drank.

GOD TESTS US

Words of testing are difficult to hear from God because tests (like confrontations and challenges) require us to know that God is the Lover of our souls, not a tyrannical wielder of thunderbolts. But testing is a part of how God educates us and forms us spiritually. Like the "discipline of the Lord" (the root word of *discipline* is related to education), testing is for our benefit: "God disciplines us for our good, that we may share in his holiness" (Hebrews 12:10). To share in His holiness? "The point of our crises and calamities is not to frighten us or beat us into submission, but to encourage us to change, to allow us to heal and grow."[4]

Expect to hear God speak to you and test you in these ways:

Look at what's in your heart. The purpose of the Israelites' forty-year wandering was to test them, "to know what was in your heart, whether or not you would keep his commands" (Deuteronomy 8:2, italics mine). Testing reveals how strong our love is for God by how eager we are to obey.

God may test the heart by asking you to give up a mission you love. In the sacrifice of Isaac, God asked Abraham not only to set aside parental-endearment and child-sacrifice issues, but also to abandon the mission God gave him—to become a great nation, which required a surviving child (see Genesis 22:2). But God wasn't interested in killing a child or disrupting a mission; He was interested in knowing Abraham's heart.

Am I enough? In good times and bad, expect to hear God asking, "Am I enough to sustain you and love you in this world?" Moses told the Israelites: "The LORD your God is testing you to find out *whether you love him with all your heart and with all your soul*" (Deuteronomy 13:3, italics mine).

When missionary Amy Carmichael was bedridden with foot problems, she hoped to be up and walking when her missionary colleague returned from furlough. Yet she wasn't even sitting in a chair. She heard the bells chime the day the colleague returned and a song came to her, beginning with these lines: "Thou has not *that,* My child, but Thou hast me, And am not I alone enough for thee?"[5]

For months, I went through a period where God seemed to be

asking me, "Am I enough? Yes, you have this and that, but am I enough?" When I despaired that I wasn't the intellect I'd love to be, God seemed to ask, "But am I enough?" When a book I'd written went out of print, I moved back and forth between clear-eyed acceptance and feeling worthless. I sensed God's question coming and wailed a favorite breath prayer, "Thou lovest me" (my old English paraphrase of John 17:23). But the question came anyway, "Am I enough?"

One day, in the quiet of contemplative prayer, I began chuckling, "More than before. I'm working on it. Any minute now You, my God, will be enough."

Through confrontations, challenges, and tests, God says difficult things to us. As we grow in a secure relationship with God, we can hear these things more easily. They sound not like cruel jibes, but like quiet, passionate reminders from the heart of God.

Always, we must remember that it is the loving parent who disciplines and directs his child. Contemplative living means living with a constant awareness that we are *children of God* (see 1 John 3:1). God makes it possible for us to receive both basic and difficult truths from Him. And this makes it possible for Him to give us the next gift—the greatest gift of all.

NOTES

1. Oswald Chambers, *My Utmost for His Highest: An Updated Edition in Today's Language*, ed. James Reimann (Grand Rapids, MI: Discovery House Publications, 1992), August 7 entry.

2. Flannery O'Connor, "The River," *O'Connor Collected Works* (New York: Literary Classics of the United States, 1988), p. 171.

3. Francis Thompson, "The Hound of Heaven," *A Treasury of Great Poems* (New York: Simon & Schuster, 1955), p. 1002. (public domain)

4. Kathleen Norris, *The Cloister Walk* (New York: Riverhead, 1996), p. 213, as quoted in Robert C. Morris, "The Second Breath: Frustration as a Doorway to Daily Spiritual Practice," *Weavings,* March/April 1998, p. 42.

5. Amy Carmichael, *A Very Present Help,* ed. Judith Couchman (Ann Arbor, MI: Servant Publications, 1996), p. 47.

CHAPTER
15

GOD REVEALS HIMSELF

G OD IS A GRACIOUS CONVERSATIONALIST. HE *WILL* TELL US ABOUT Himself, which helps us build a relationship in which we trust Him with everything we've got. As we get to know the heart of God, we're more likely to refuse temptation because we love God too much to give in.

What can bind us to the heart of God so that, ultimately, nothing can tear us away from Him for long? In this chapter, we will see how we come to know the heart of God through watching Him grieve, going through "desert" experiences with Him, and receiving the intimacy He offers. These experiences help us live in the reality that we are bound to the heart of God.

GOD GRIEVES

In the silence of contemplative prayer, the pain of others may come to the front of our minds. We may weep for the pain of a child's abuse, the bombing of a faraway city, or an injustice in our neighborhood. Poet Gerard Manley Hopkins described it this way: "The Holy Ghost over the bent world broods."[1]

To sit with God and let one's heart be broken by the things that break the heart of God results in a selfless heart for others. Jean-Nicholas Grou had such a heart. When I've quoted him, it's been from his book *How to Pray*, written while he was in exile. As he wrote it, he wept over the sad state of the clergy in France, the church in France, and the government of France.[2] If I'd been him, I would have been crying over my exile. But Grou knew the heart of God and cried God's tears.

In contemplation, you are likely to hear God grieve for reasons such as these:

Grief over the destruction of people. Isaiah expressed overwhelming grief this way: "Turn away from me; let me weep bitterly. Do not try to console me over the destruction of my people" (Isaiah 22:4). The prophet Jeremiah had similar words: "My eyes fail from weeping, I am in torment within, my heart is poured out on the ground because my people are destroyed, because children and infants faint in the streets of the city" (Lamentations 2:11). In the silence, the passions of God touch us and we join God in His tears.

Pain over the wickedness of people. Christians today talk about how they don't watch the evening news or read the newspaper to avoid exposure to worldliness, but the media can be a good place to learn to cry God's tears over the wickedness on earth. If you see with the eyes of God's heart, things look different because of His pain. When questioned about God's supposed capriciousness, Madeleine L'Engle replies, "Humanity became so wicked that God cried forty days and forty nights."[3] The Flood was about punishment, but it was also God's grief over the choices of people.

Imagine the "grief of the Holy Spirit of God," which results from our "bitterness, rage and anger, brawling and slander" (Ephesians 4:30-31). How does God feel, I wonder, after a rancorous church board meeting? After two friends have quarreled? After a teen is arrested? These verses point to the heartbreak God feels when followers of Jesus choose to dabble in bitterness, rage, and slander.

Grief over pain as people suffer consequences. If I express grief at someone being in prison or going through a divorce, people often say, "Well, he deserved it." Does that response sum up the heart of God? I don't think so, based on how God behaved in the midst of administering a punishment to Israel determined by their king himself.

God grieved and told "the angel who was destroying the people, 'Enough! Withdraw your hand'" (1 Chronicles 21:15).

One woman experienced God's grief while visiting the German concentration camp Treblinka. She was stunned by the silence of acres of stones and a large monument at this former Nazi gas chamber. She described it as an urgent screaming silence, a silence of the absent voices of one million murdered Jewish men, women, and children who had been systematically gassed there with calculated efficiency in less than two years time. She also talked about the larger, louder silence of God—an anguished silent Power. This silence of God is "not passive, but a powerful response to humankind's [behavior]. Yet in this awful silence, God is present, wounded but undefeated. I experienced God's presence as Outraged Presence, divine anger at the mind-boggling offense that took place there, based on God's infinite love for life, for people, for creation."[4]

We join God in that outrage and grief, often in silent wordless prayer. And then, God is likely to call us to "places" in our spiritual life where we have never gone—and perhaps would never choose to go. And in this, there is a partnership with God's purpose.

GOD'S SILENCE LEADS US TO THE DESERT

We prefer to ponder the God who consoles us, but there are times we also experience what seems like abandonment by God. Intellectually, we understand God is omnipresent, but God seems somehow distant.

In these moments, we thirst for God, but God doesn't seem to be found: "As the deer pants for streams of water, so my soul pants for you, O God. My soul thirsts for God, for the living God. When can I go and meet with God? My tears have been my food day and night, while men say to me all day long, 'Where is your God?' I say to God my Rock, 'Why have you forgotten me?'" (Psalm 42:1-3,9). This psalm presents the dryness and insecurity of a soul living in the desert, wanting to hear from God, but sensing only abandonment.

So it is that we may encounter:

God's long pauses. Consider how one mother, begging deliverance for her daughter, experienced long pauses from Jesus: "A Canaanite woman from that vicinity came to him, crying out, 'Lord,

Son of David, have mercy on me! My daughter is suffering terribly from demon-possession.' *Jesus did not answer a word"* (Matthew 15:22-23, italics mine).

What did this Gentile woman experience when Jesus did not speak to her or notice her? Why did Jesus pause? Helmut Thielicke writes, "Jesus is at first silent in the face of her request: 'He answered her not a word.' The silence of God is the greatest test of our faith."[5]

When Jesus finally did respond by stating His purpose (to be for the Jews first), "there is outcry and gesticulation [on her part]. The need is laid before God. Then there is silence. There are dangerous pauses. There are moments when understanding breaks off, when crises arise, when it seems any moment as though one or the other will get up and go. Silence, rejection, pauses, acceptance—all have their place in this dialogue [with God]."[6]

Why was Jesus so reticent? Eventually He would heal this woman's daughter and compliment her faith! As Thielicke continues:

The silence of God is different from that of [humans].
When Jesus lay silent and asleep in the ship, He was more
kind and His arm was more near to help and more certain
than the anxious cry of the doubting disciples suggests.
The silence of God and of Jesus is not of indifference. It is
the silence of higher thoughts. God is fitting stone to stone
in His plan for the world and our lives, even though we
can see only a confused and meaningless jumble of stones
heaped together under a silent heaven.[7]

God's silence—often called our "desert experience"—can happen to anyone. An acquaintance of mine who is a music minister at a large church wrote to tell me, "It's ironic for me to think that the desert would be in the midst of a job that many would envy."

Being in the desert is not bad or abnormal. Jeremiah and Ezekiel, who both obeyed God faithfully, experienced the desert and didn't hurry it away. "Every drop of gall of this divine bitterness must be drained to the dregs to the point of intoxication," writes Jean-Pierre de Caussade. "Jeremiah and Ezekiel, whose only words were tears and sighs, could never find consolation except in continual lamentations. He who would have stopped the flow of their tears would have removed the most beautiful parts of the scriptures."[8]

We dislike the desert because, seemingly unlike Jeremiah and Ezekiel, we want to fix things quickly and to make life beautiful and harmonious again. The desert, however, is not a problem to be solved but a mysterious place to dwell for a while.

A time of purifying. At a point in my life that seemed like a spiritual dead end, I frequently walked in the cemetery near my home. I cried out. I sat on the tombstones in silence; at times, I laid face down on them. It seemed like God was absent. I now understand this was a turning point in my spiritual life, a purifying of the soul in the desert. It wasn't that God wanted me to be miserable, but He wanted me back—with a new and different spirit.

That portion of my journey resembled the classic "dark night of the soul," which is filled with a sense of abandonment. The soul seems dried out. The pleasure of the devotional life is gone. This is different from depression or grief, although we may go through them at the same time. In this void, nothing works and there is little joy. As the purification of the soul occurs, we discover we've been seeking the consolation of God for the sake of His consolation. It wasn't God we loved as much as His ability to solve problems and fix our world.

The "dark night" is often the disease of those who are too spiritual—talking about spiritual things all the time, preferring to teach rather than be taught, and condemning others who aren't as spiritual as they are. The dark night stops us and purifies us before our great love for spiritual things turns into self-satisfaction, spiritual greed, and spiritual gluttony.[9]

In that dark night season I began reading regularly *The Practice of the Presence of God* by Brother Lawrence. I can see now where I underlined heavily the phrase that "I desire Him to form His perfect image on my soul."[10] That was my goal in those days—to be like God rather than to love God. Gradually, I realized that my spirituality was about *me*. The music minister I mentioned on the previous page recognized that his spirituality was drenched in self as well: "I've fasted and prayed, probably pushing too hard for concrete words of direction from God. I've forgotten how to really savor those quiet moments in His presence."

In this purifying time, we discover that our joy in life is based on money, relationships, career, or family, but all these are transient. The joy of living must be based in knowing God.

> Abram went through thirteen years of silence, but in those years all of his self-sufficiency was destroyed. He grew past the point of relying on his own common sense. Those years of silence were a time of discipline, not a time of God's displeasure. There is never any need to pretend that your life is filled with joy and confidence; just wait upon God and be grounded in Him.[11]

The dark nights and desert days become places in which we learn to rest in the silence of God and no longer fear them. Psalm 42 offers no suggestions for what you might hear from God. That's the point. What we hear at times is blank silence. Wordless contemplation is also a way to connect with God at this time. No words, just "being."

But Psalm 42 does present images to rest in: a thirsty deer, tears as food, God as rock, pouring out the soul, being swept by waves. Images help. It was during my dark night that I began going to art museums and collecting art books to peruse. Images without words expressed my condition, and looking at art seemed like prayer to me. At that time, I bought a miniature of Michelangelo's *Pietà*. It portrays a piece of the desert I will never lose — being held as Jesus was, except I am in the arms of God, broken and spilled out, but receiving the careful attention of the Father.

GOD OFFERS US INTIMACY

God gazes on us with love, even in the midst of challenges (see Mark 10:21). The psalmist who had gotten himself tangled in the ocean's cords of death was rescued by God and said, "He brought me out into a spacious place; he rescued me because he delighted in me" (Psalm 18:19). To a nation about to undergo tragedy and destruction and eventually restoration, God said, "The LORD your God is with you, he is mighty to save. He will take great delight in you, he will quiet you with his love, he will rejoice over you with singing" (Zephaniah 3:17). As if rocking us in His lap and cooing over us quietly,

God does not withdraw love—even though we're sure He has. In the words of Julian of Norwich, "Betwixt God and me there is no between."[12]

What we can expect to hear from God in the quiet of contemplative prayer are the words "I am with you," "I delight in you," "I see your faults and invite you to come to Me." "Prayer," says Thomas Merton, "especially meditation and contemplative prayer, is not so much a way to find God as a way of resting in him who we have found, who loves us, who is near to us, who comes to us to draw us to himself."[13]

Once while meditating on Jesus' image of the treasure buried in the field (see Matthew 13:44)—the one a person would sell everything to obtain—I heard myself listing the desirable things that the buried treasure was not: becoming a great writer, having good relationships with my children. Then I opened my eyes and gasped in surprise, "Oh, God, I get it. The treasure is You! I knew this, but now I taste it, see it, hear it in a way that has escaped me in the past. You are enough." We are sure God wants us to believe right things, and very sure He wants to use us as His servants. But in the end, the sweetest gift He will give us—if we are open—is the gift of Himself.

My goal has been to invite you to "taste and see that the LORD is good" (Psalm 34:8). One of the ways we can do this is to set out on the contemplative way. God will meet you there, speaking to you in His Word and by the Holy Spirit. My prayer is that we, God's children, will learn to receive God in every part of our lives and that He will then transform us into the light of the world (see Matthew 5:14), quiet bonfires of the life of God who dwells in us. That is what's needed by a world that God *so loves*.

NOTES

1. Gerard Manley Hopkins, "God's Grandeur," *The Works of Gerard Manley Hopkins* (Hertfordshire, England: Wordsworth Poetry Library, 1994), p. 26.
2. Jean-Nicholas Grou, *How to Pray* (Cambridge, England: James Clarke & Co., 1955), p. 120.
3. I heard Madeleine L'Engle say this at a retreat, February 17, 1998.
4. Elaine V. Emeth, "Lessons from the Holocaust: Living Faithfully in the Midst of Chaos," *Weavings*, March/April 1998, pp. 18-19.

5. Helmut Thielicke, "The Silence of God," *Cross Point*, Summer 1997, p. 34.

6. Thielicke, p. 34.

7. Thielicke, p. 36.

8. Jean-Pierre de Caussade, *The Sacrament of the Present Moment* (San Francisco: Harper & Row, 1982), p. 96.

9. John of the Cross, *Renovaré Devotional Readings, ed.* James B. Smith, vol. 1, no. 45 (Wichita, KS: Renovaré, 1990, looseleaf notebook edition), p. 1, "Secret Pride."

10 Brother Lawrence, *The Practice of the Presence of God* (Old Tappan, NJ: Fleming H. Revell, 1958), pp. 37-38.

11. Oswald Chambers, *My Utmost for His Highest: An Updated Edition in Today's Language*, ed. James Reimann (Grand Rapids, MI: Discovery House Publications, 1992), January 19 entry.

12. As quoted by Wendy M. Wright, "Wisdom of the Mothers," *Weavings,* July/August 1997, p. 17.

13. Thomas Merton, *Contemplative Prayer* (New York: Doubleday, An Image Book, 1996), p. 29.

EPILOGUE

IN THIS BOOK, I HAVE OUTLINED ONE OF THE MANY PATHS AVAILABLE to you in the spiritual formation of your soul. My prayer for you is that this book will help "nourish in your heart a lively longing for God."[1]

As that happens, expect some interesting changes. "The contemplative life is that radical and risky opening of self to be changed by God. It causes us to see beyond our present seeing. Thus it is a life of continual dying, of being stripped over and over again of the comfortable and familiar, a life of letting go and allowing a reality beyond our own to shape us."[2] That openness to God will cause soul-growth. Here are some types of growth that are likely to occur:

Accepting all things. Spiritual formation helps us trust God enough to accept circumstances and abandon our attempts to manage and control our world. "Abandonment is casting off all your cares. Abandonment is dropping all your needs. It is leaving the future in His hands. Abandonment is being satisfied with the present moment, no matter what that moment contains."[3] When I pray "Into Thy hands" (an abbreviation of Jesus' words on the cross), I can view a situation in God's hands, making it easier to accept and more likely that I'll move through it with grace.

Simplicity. Focusing on God makes the voices of our culture less deafening, and so simplicity of speech and lifestyle come more naturally. Maybe I can live in a smaller house or wear clothes that are ten years old or not have to have the last word in every situation. The value of things fades because you're living more in the unseen world, and what is unseen—that delightful COMPANIONSHIP with God—is worth more than a house with a three-car garage with three overwhelming cars in it.

Singleness of heart. In silence, we hear our motives and inner voices and recognize how they draw us away from God. We long to live with an undivided heart (see Psalm 86:11), described well by Henri Nouwen:

> When my heart is undivided, my mind only concerned
> about God, my soul full of his love, everything comes
> together into one perspective and nothing remains excluded.
> For the first time I sensed a real single-mindedness; my
> mind seemed to expand and to be able to receive endlessly
> more than when I feel divided and confused.[4]

These are the ways a nourished heart behaves. May your heart find nourishment in God.

My insights on contemplative prayer are still evolving. As you walk your journey with God, I'd love to hear how God is doing the work of spiritual formation in you. Please write and tell me what you're learning.

Jan Johnson
NavPress
P. O. Box 35001
Colorado Springs, CO 80935

NOTES
1. Fr. James Walsh, ed., *The Cloud of Unknowing* (Rahwey, NJ: Paulist Press, 1981), p. 47.
2. Wendy Wright, "Contemplation in Time of War," *Weavings*, July/August 1992, p. 22.
3. Jeanne Guyon, *Experiencing the Depths of Jesus Christ* (Beaumont, TX: The SeedSowers, 1975), pp. 34-35.
4. Henri Nouwen, *The Genesee Diary: Report from a Trappist Monastery* (New York: Doubleday, An Image Book, 1989), pp. 141-142.

AUTHOR

JAN JOHNSON is the author of more than ten books that deal with building an authentic life with God and the use of spiritual disciplines. These books include *Enjoying the Presence of God* (NavPress), which focuses on practicing God's presence and *Listening to God* (NavPress), which focuses on Scripture meditation. Besides writing, Jan speaks frequently at retreats and conferences. She earned her degree in Christian education and has written more than 700 Bible studies. A trained spiritual director, Jan desires to help believers immerse themselves in life with God. She lives with her family in Simi, California.

GENERAL EDITOR

DALLAS WILLARD is a professor in the school of philosophy at the University of Southern California in Los Angeles. He has been at USC since 1965, where he was director of the school of philosophy from 1982 to 1985. He has also taught at the University of Wisconsin (Madison), where he received his Ph.D. in 1964, and has held visiting appointments at UCLA (1969) and the University of Colorado (1984).

His philosophical publications are mainly in the areas of epistemology, the philosophy of mind and of logic, and on the philosophy of Edmund Husserl, including extensive translations of Husserl's early writings from German into English. His *Logic and the Objectivity of Knowledge*, a study on Husserl's early philosophy, appeared in 1984.

Dr. Willard also lectures and publishes in religion. *In Search of Guidance* was published in 1984 (second edition in 1993), and *The Spirit of the Disciplines* was released in 1988.

He is married to Jane Lakes Willard, a marriage and family counselor with offices in Van Nuys and Canoga Park, California. They have two children, John and Rebecca, and live in Chatsworth, California.

EDITOR

DAVID HAZARD is the editor of spiritual formation books for NavPress. He is also the editor of the classic devotional series, *Rekindling the Inner Fire*, and writes the monthly column, "Classic Christianity" for *Charisma* magazine.

For more than seventeen years, David has held various positions with Christian publishing houses, from editorial director to associate publisher. As a writer, he has contributed numerous internationally bestselling books to contemporary Christian publishing, some of which have been published in more than twenty languages worldwide. As an editor, David has developed more than two hundred books.

For the past twelve years, his special focus and study has been in the classic writings of Christianity, the formation of early Christian doctrine, and Christian spirituality.